400 YE
OF
THE WE

A history of Tunbridge Wells

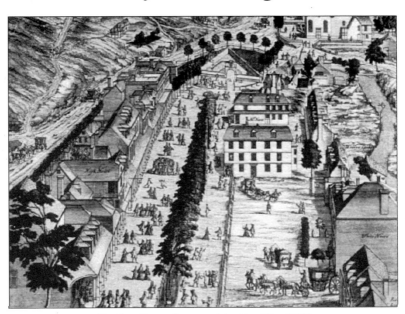

The Pantiles – Engraved by Jan Kip, 1719

by
Members of the Local History Group
of the
Royal Tunbridge Wells Civic Society

Foreword by the Marquess of Abergavenny and the Earl of Guilford

Edited by John Cunningham

Royal Tunbridge Wells Civic Society
Local History Monograph No. 5
2005

ROYAL
TUNBRIDGE 4
WELLS

**Published in Great Britain in October 2005 by
The Local History Group of
The Royal Tunbridge Wells Civic Society**

Second impression April 2008

ISBN 0-9545343-5-2

The text is set in Bookman Old Style 10 pt.
and the front cover in Bookman Old Style 8-30 pt.

Front cover: Frontispiece of 'Tunbridge Wells; or, A Day's Courtship',
a comedy by Thomas Rawlins, 1678
Back cover: Church of King Charles the Martyr
Title page: The Pantiles – engraved by Jan Kip, 1719.

Printed and bound by The Ink Pot Lithographic Printers,
Southborough, Tunbridge Wells, Kent TN4 0LT

CONTENTS

'Taking the Waters' – the origin of Tunbridge Wells – in the early 20th century.

FOREWORD

by

The Marquess of Abergavenny
and the Earl of Guilford

It gives us great pleasure to introduce this new history of Tunbridge Wells, produced to mark the 400th Anniversary of the discovery of the Wells in 1606 by our ancestors, the 3rd Lord North and the 6th Baron Bergavenny.

It is an interesting thought that without their relatively chance discovery, the very pleasant and attractive town of Tunbridge Wells might never have existed, which would have been a great loss to the world; and in some respects, the course of history might have been changed.

We have read this history with great interest and although familiar with much of it, we must also admit that we have learnt much. We commend it to the reader.

Christopher Nevill
6th. Marquess of Abergavenny

Piers North
10th. Earl of Guilford

September, 2005

1

Tunbridge Wells humbly Dedicated to Thomas Pellet. M.D.

Engraving of Tunbridge Wells by Jan Kip. 1719.

INTRODUCTION

Tunbridge Wells has benefited from a number of excellent histories, from the original one by Benge Burr in 1766, to John Britton's 'Descriptive Sketches' in 1832, Lewis Melville's 'Society at Tunbridge Wells in the 18th Century and After' in 1912, Margaret Barton's 'Tunbridge Wells' in 1937, Alan Savidge's 'Royal Tunbridge Wells' in 1975 and Roger Farthing's 'Mount Sion' in 2003.

Some of these histories were inevitably limited in their coverage of the past 400 years by their date of publication; others by the author's choice of a specific subject. Even the most recent 'comprehensive' history by Alan Savidge understandably skated over the latter half of the 20th. century, probably on the grounds that the events were known to everybody and needed little explanation, or that it was in any case too early to assess the implications of what had happened so recently.

However, now that we are approaching the Fourth Centenary of the discovery of the Wells in 1606, without which Royal Tunbridge Wells would not exist, the Local History Group of the Royal Tunbridge Wells Civic Society thought that it was appropriate to mark the Centenary by publishing a new and comprehensive history of Tunbridge Wells in its Local History Monograph series, which would not only update, but maybe give a new perspective on the Town and its development.

This Monograph is different from all the previous histories, insofar as it is written not by one person, but by several – some eight members of the Local History Group, many with a specialist knowledge of their period and its issues, but all with very differing styles and approaches. It is therefore by its nature, essentially a series of essays by different authors, in broadly chronological sequence, about the 400 years since the discovery of the Wells. The Editor has not sought to curb these differences or impose any form of straight-jacket on style, but he has sought to remove undue overlap and fill in obvious omissions.

The first two chapters explain, first, the geological and industrial background of the Weald without which the Weald could never have existed or been developed; and second, the historical attitude to wells and spas since Roman times; and the particular English attitude to them in the 16th century prior to the discovery of the Wells at Tunbridge in 1606.

The Royal Tunbridge Wells Civic Society would like to thank the Marquess of Abergavenny and the Earl of Guilford for their kind Foreword; and the Tunbridge Wells Borough Council for their financial guarantee in the production of this Monograph.

CHAPTER 1

THE ORIGINS OF THE HIGH WEALD AND ITS IRON INDUSTRY

by John Cunningham

The site of Tunbridge Wells lies at the heart of the Weald of Kent and Sussex.

The Weald owes its name to the Saxon and Jutish settlers who came between 450-700 AD, and who used the German word 'wald' meaning 'wood or forest', to describe the area.

The Anglo-Saxon Chronicle of 893 AD gives the extent of this forest as 120 miles east to west and 30 miles north to south, although some reservations may be expressed about the accuracy of the Chronicle's means of measurement.

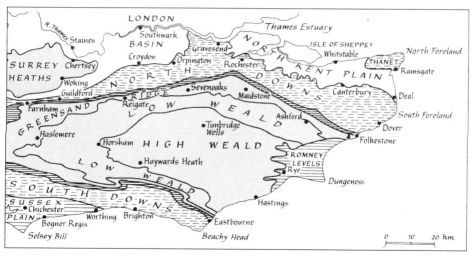

The Weald

Designed by John Talbot White and drawn by Neil Hyslop.

The Weald extends over parts of four counties – Kent, Sussex, Surrey and Hampshire – and is a large mainly oval ridge of over 1,000 square miles, at its widest about 70 miles east to west, and 40 miles north to south; and it is bounded by the North and South Downs. It is convex, or hump-backed rather like an upturned rowing boat, with the High Weald representing the keel and bottom; and its many small valleys (or ghylls, as they are called locally), the overlapping planks of the bottom.

4

The Weald was not always convex or hump-backed. Indeed its origin was the reverse. At the end of the Jurassic Period, about 140 million years ago, the area was a concave freshwater/brackish swamp, or lake, that was sinking faster than the deposits of mud, silt and sand that came from the rivers and streams draining into it. This situation continued for at least 20 million years of the Cretaceous Period (which was between 140-65 million years ago). This subsidence spread to the surrounding land, so much so that nearly all of what is now the British Isles and much of the Continent was submerged under the sea.

During this period, the Weald had a warm climate and dinosaurs roamed across it. Deposits continued to be laid down, whether under water, or in swamp, or on land subject to flooding; and the varying strata of deposits can be easily identified. The bottom stratum, now called the Purbeck Beds, was laid down in Jurassic times. Those laid down in the Cretaceous Period are called the Wealden Beds and are classified further into Hastings Beds, which are broken down further into Ashdown Beds, Wadhurst Clay, Tunbridge Wells Sand and Weald Clay. The total thickness of the Wealden Beds sediment alone is estimated at 2,000 feet.

However, at the end of the Cretaceous Period, some 65 million years ago, subsidence gave way to uplift and the Central Weald rose to emerge above sea-level early in the Tertiary Period (65–2 million years ago). The deposits of mud, silt and sand had been compressed into layers of clay, setstone and sandstone and, with their emergence above water, a slow process of weathering and erosion set in, removing the tops of layers to differing degrees, and slowly creating the topography of the Weald as we know it today.

In those days, the geology of the Weald extended (and still extends) into what is now France, since the English Channel had not yet been formed. That geology can be seen around Boulogne, Dieppe and Beauvais, although now separated from the Weald by the English Channel, which was created through a relatively swift inundation from the North Sea, which made Britain an island a mere 8,000 years ago.

The Wealden Beds contain significant deposits of clay ironstone (siderite ferrous carbonate, $FeCO_3$), the raw material of iron manufacture, and the iron in the ironstone would have been deposited in Cretaceous times, at least 65 million years before. It was this ironstone that provided the raw material that made the Weald the industrial centre of England in two periods – the Roman Empire and again in the 14th-17th centuries.

The importance of iron to society and its influence on the development of society, cannot be over-estimated. Iron was not only essential for tools – axes, hammers, knives, razors, nails, cleavers – but also for everyday needs such as locks, keys, hinges and horseshoes – and weapons – swords, daggers, lances, arrow heads, shields, helmets and armour.

The Weald had the ideal combination for the production of iron – an ample supply of raw material, iron ore, that was near the surface and easy to mine; and a vast forest to provide the charcoal that was the most important fuel in the ancient world and essential to achieve the temperatures of 900 – 1600°F necessary for iron-making.

The size of the Weald Iron Industry should not be under-estimated. There are today 527 known sites in the Weald for bloomery (i.e. direct reduction) iron-making and 76 of them are of Roman origin.

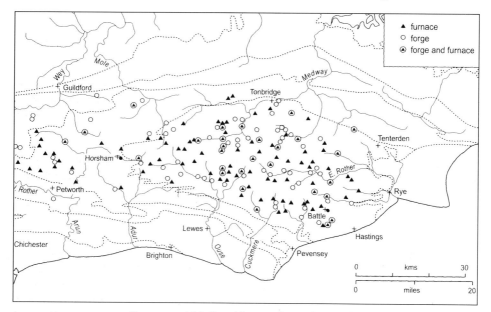

Roman and Medieval Ironworks in the Weald.

From Roman times until the 15th century, the only method of smelting iron ore was the direct method, or 'bloomery' process, which heated the iron to a temperature below that at which it melts, but high enough to remove 'slag' (unwanted minerals), which can be vapourised, liquefied and drained. At the same time, the gas produced by the charcoal creates a chemical reaction with the ore to reduce it to iron, as a sponge-like 'bloom', capable of further refining.

The 'bloomery' process is not very efficient and the growing Weald Iron Industry was to benefit considerably between 1490 and 1540 from the introduction of new technology from the Continent and particularly from French iron-workers who were brought over and settled. This new process was a more efficient system called the indirect method, in which liquid iron is produced in a blast furnace at a high temperature and then further refined in a finery forge.

As a result, the Weald Iron Industry prospered until the late 17th century (well after the discovery of the Wells in 1606). But it was then to fall on hard times, partly because of an increasing shortage of charcoal as the vast Weald forest was consumed in charcoal production, but more importantly in the early 18th century by the discovery in 1709 by Abraham Darby of the method of converting coal into coke. Coke was much more efficient than charcoal in the production of iron; and coal was more widely available.

The Weald Iron Industry was doomed, but it took quite a long time dying and lingered on until 1828 when the last furnace closed at Ashburnham; and the Weald reverted to the countryside we all know.

A major (although relatively indirect) player in the Industry would have been the Bergavenny or Nevill family, who were leading landowners in the area and who, therefore, would have had ultimate control of much of the Industry.

Originally the family title was Lord (of) Bergavenny (a title created in 1450), but this was changed by the 14th Baron in 1734 to Abergavenny. (His heir, the 15th Baron, subsequently became the first Earl of Abergavenny in 1784; and a later descendant, the 5th Earl, became the 1st Marquess just under a century later in 1876.)

But more important than the family title is the family name, Nevill. The Nevill family with its many branches has played a major part in English history since at least the 12th century. They were the most powerful family in England during the 15th century with Warwick the Kingmaker the head of the family, making and unmaking kings during the Wars of the Roses.

Before 1500, branches of the family held a great number of titles:

❖ the Dukedom of Bedford,
❖ the Marquessate of Montagu,
❖ the Earldoms of Westmoreland, Salisbury, Warwick, Kent and Northumberland,

❖ and the Baronies of Nevill, Furnivall, Latymer, Fauconberg and Bergavenny.

The Nevills did not settle in Sussex until the mid-15th century when Sir Edward Nevill, KG, youngest brother of Warwick the Kingmaker, married his second cousin, Lady Elisabeth Beauchamp, the only child of Richard Beauchamp, Earl of Worcester and Lord of Bergavenny, who owned much land in the Weald. As a result, the Nevill family in the Weald benefited from the rise of the iron industry during the 15th, 16th, and 17th centuries, when the Weald became the English industrial centre of its time – the Black Country of the Middle Ages, as it has been called.

The Nevill family had been visited at Eridge for six days in August 1573 by Queen Elizabeth, but it was not then their principal residence, reputedly because of the noise and smoke of iron-making at Eridge.

There was an additional but highly relevant side-benefit for the Nevills from the Weald's geology and industry, which took them and others some time to be recognise; and certainly not before 1606.

To us today, it is not surprising that an iron-producing area should also have chalybeate springs i.e. springs whose water is heavily impregnated with iron.

Even at the turn of the 16th/17th centuries, it would only be a matter of time before this would be discovered, recognised and valued; and the Bergavenny family was to play its part in this, as well.

CHAPTER 2

BATHS, HOLY WELLS AND SPAS

by John Cunningham

The practice of bathing for medical reasons in thermal (i.e. natural, hot) springs dates from at least Roman times and was widespread in Europe. In Britain, the two prime locations for it were Bath (called Aquae Sulis) and Buxton (Aquae Arnemetiae).

The practice of drinking, or applying, the water, to parts of the body for medical reasons from natural but cold springs is more difficult to date, but probably was co-existent with bathing in hot-springs.

As the Roman Empire declined, the use of springs for bathing diminished as did hygiene and personal cleanliness generally, but they continued to exist, being subsumed into the Christian religion as 'holy wells', often dedicated to Our Lady, or a local Saint. The medicinal or healing qualities of their waters were translated into miraculous powers which made them a place of pilgrimage, particularly in the Middle Ages.

At the English Reformation which began in 1535, the 'holy wells', of which there were an estimated 450 in England alone, were suppressed as 'religious superstition', under the orders of Henry VIII and his henchman, Thomas Cromwell. The suppression was not entirely successful, since many ordinary people were loath to abandon what had been part of their cultural, social and religious heritage for so long.

However by the accession of Elizabeth I in 1558, the situation had changed somewhat. The Acts of Supremacy and Uniformity of 1559 forced those who still held with the 'old' religion, to conform, or else suffer fine and/or imprisonment. As a result, English Catholic recusants began to leave the country ostensibly for health reasons, and particularly for Spa, a town in the Ardennes, well-known in England since about 1540 for its healing waters. But the real worry for Elizabeth and her advisers was that the Ardennes (now in Belgium) were then in the Spanish Netherlands; and all English visitors there were suspected by the English Crown of being Catholic dissidents and plotting with Spain and the Pope against Elizabeth.

So to discourage any need to go abroad the prohibitions about visiting/using the English wells were withdrawn; and the exodus to Spa was controlled by an Act of 1571 which required all foreign travel to be authorised by licence, that is by a system of passports for which justification had to be provided by the applicant. At broadly the same time, a more secular and 'scientific' approach to the benefits of mineral waters began to be published, which went a long way to counteracting the previous religious context.

So a combination of restrictions on travel abroad without detailed justification, together with a medical/medicinal rationale of the benefits of mineral water springs, both combined to begin the practice of the English nobility and gentry taking medication and relaxation in an English inland watering place. These presented new and unique opportunities for informal social intercourse, for the exchange of ideas and opinions, and for intrigue and gossip, away from the Court in London. They were the beginnings of the concept of a holiday as we know it today – but only for the upper classes.

The number of Spas (or 'Spaws', as they were originally known) grew and in the late 16th. century there was almost a mania for well-finding. Many wells were previously 'holy wells' now restored to favour with or without 'scientific' backing, but new ones kept being found. Harrogate, initially a purely drinking spa rather than a bathing one, was discovered in 1571, but got off to a fairly shaky start. However, it recovered in the late 17th. century. Kings Newnham, between Coventry and Rugby and not far from the later site of Royal Leamington Spa, was discovered in 1579 and made a good start. But it was a cold water spring (unlike Bath with three springs between 117-120°F, and Buxton [then known as Buckstones] with nine springs at 82°F), and its coldness probably did not suit the English temperament in the long-run.

The principal Spas of Bath and Buxton received Royal approval and this set the stamp of fashion on them. Elizabeth I visited Bath for five days in August 1574, although there is no record of her actually 'taking the waters' as did many subsequent visitors. Her Progress, planned to include Bath in July 1602, had to be abandoned due to bad weather and ill-health. But her first cousin, Mary Queen of Scots, was permitted to visit Buxton no fewer than nine times between 1573-1584, despite being detained/imprisoned in Wingfield Manor, Derby and Fotheringay Castle, during this time.

So the social, intellectual and political climate was entirely favourable to Spas, and the discovery of new Spas. Which may explain why the discovery of a new well, six miles south of the ancient town of Tunbridge, on the northern edge of the Ashdown Forest, and only 35 miles from

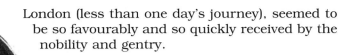

London (less than one day's journey), seemed to be so favourably and so quickly received by the nobility and gentry.

Dudley, 3rd Lord North.

The two principals involved – Dudley, 3rd Lord North and Edward, 6th Lord Bergavenny – were very familiar with Spas. Lord North's grandfather (Roger, the 2nd. Lord) had visited Buxton once (in 1578) and Bath three times (1589, 1594, and 1600), dying in 1600; Lord North, who succeeded his grandfather, had visited Spa in 1602; and Lord Bergavenny had been to Bath in 1595. So they were not ingénues as far as Spas were concerned.

The relationship of Lord Bergavenny and Lord North is not defined in any detail in any description of the discovery of the Wells. Certainly they must have been friends, otherwise why was Lord North staying with Lord Bergavenny. But they were not the same age. In 1606, Lord North was 25 and Lord Bergavenny must have been about 56, so the friendship may have been more social than personal. Lord Bergavenny only survived another 16 years, dying at the age of about 72, while Lord North was to live for another 60 years, dying at the age of 85 in 1666.

The site of the Wells which they discovered, is somewhat problematic since its position is at the junction of:

two County boundaries (Kent and Sussex),

two Manor boundaries (Rusthall and South Frith)

and three Parish boundaries (Speldhurst, Tonbridge, and Frant);

and this has provided many opportunities for disagreement, or even conflict, over the intervening years.

Parish boundary mark in the pavement by King Charles the Martyr, Tunbridge Wells.

CHAPTER 3

THE QUEEN'S WELLS

by Philip Whitbourn

It is from the "recovery of an eminent nobleman", observed Tunbridge Wells' first historian, Thomas Benge Burr in the mid 18th century, "that we must date all the honours to which Tunbridge Wells has risen." Benge Burr then went on to add that "if we trace its story to the head, it will appear that so trifling an incident as the colour of the ground about the water of a wild and unuseful wood, has filled the desert with inhabitants, and made plenty smile over the barren heath."[1]

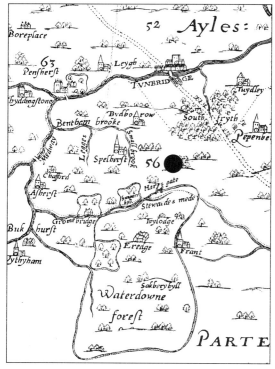

Detail from Symondson's Map of Kent 1596, indicating the approximate location of the future Royal Tunbridge Wells.

The "eminent nobleman" to whom Benge Burr was referring was Dudley, third Baron North (1581-1666), a conspicuous figure at court in his time. The "trifling ... incident" mentioned by Benge Burr was that of Lord North chancing upon an ochreous spring between Lord Bergavenny's Eridge estate in Sussex where he had been staying for health reasons, and the town of Tonbridge in Kent. The reference to a "wild and unuseful wood" and to the "barren heath" relate, of course, to the once largely uninhabited stretch of land between the Hargate to Waterdown Forest and South Frith, as shown on Symondson's map of 1596, where now is situated the post-medieval historic spa town of Royal Tunbridge Wells. Despite the blank patch on Symondson's map, it is known from archaeological investigations, such as those at High Rocks, that early man had a presence in the area.

Moreover, it seems likely that the health-giving spring was known to local inhabitants in Elizabethan or earlier times, as a Tudor map of the area survives in the National Archives at Kew.[2] This shows the districts of South Frith to the north and of Waterdown to the South, with the Kent county boundary marked in between. In Tudor times the hunting park at South Frith was enclosed with a pale, or fence, through which a gate, significantly marked "Wel Spryngate", opened on to a "highway" leading southwards towards the county boundary, and in the direction of the area that we now know as The Pantiles, to the north of Broadwater Down. The map seems to have been produced in connection with arguments over land claimed by one Anthony Wybarne, sometime a tenant of the Duke of Buckingham[3], which need not trouble us here. However, the map does show a few houses in elevation, indicating that there was probably some modest form of human activity in the area before Lord North came upon the scene. Benge Burr mentions Lord North as ordering one of his attendants to borrow a little vessel from a neighbouring dwelling, believed to be that of Mrs Humphreys, the Wells' first "dipper".

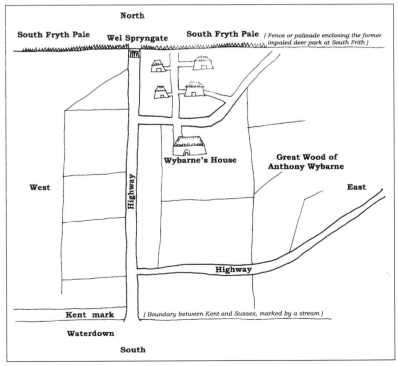

Transcription of the Tudor map in the National Archives, showing the area between South Frith and Waterdown.

To attempt any definitive interpretation of this Tudor map could be a contentious business. The map is one of a set of three maps that are preserved in the National Archives at Kew. All three show the same area, but in varying degrees of detail and with some inconsistencies between them. Furthermore, the Old Legal Hand script with which the maps are annotated, is sometimes obscure, even when the text is in English rather than Latin; and interpretation and understanding is not helped by the fact that at the time of the map being drawn, our convention of putting north at the top was not yet established and so in this particular case, north happens to be at the bottom of the map. The redrawn map, illustrated here, puts north at the top, with the result that the road layout looks much more like those illustrated by Seller in 1680 and Hasted in the 18th century.

With this orientation, it does seem likely that the north-south 'Highway' shown on the map was the road to Southborough, which we would now call Mount Pleasant Road and the High Street. Off this north-south axis, east-west roads, apparently in the vicinity of the present Crescent Road and Mount Sion, are shown leading north-eastwards in the direction of Pembury. If this hypothesis is correct, then it might be that 'Wybarne's House ' was a forerunner of the old Calverley House on Mount Pleasant, and thus of the present 'Hotel du Vin' building.

The maps appear to show the name of Wybarne's House as "Bromelerige". Bromele might possibly signify a heath or meadow where Brome grass grows and, certainly, there is a ridge at the top of the Wells hill and along the northern skyline of the Calverley Grounds. Be that as it may, there can be little doubt that the elevation illustrating Wybarne's House indicates a crenellated or battlemented parapet, suggesting that the building was more than a mere cottage.

While therefore heath and woodland no doubt predominated in this area in late Elizabethan times, it would seem that the place was not quite the wilderness which has sometimes been suggested, and it could be that the ground-plan of what was to become the Tunbridge Wells town centre of today, was already being laid down before the Wells were even 'discovered'. However, without Lord North passing that way in the early years of King James I's reign, that ground-plan could never have developed in the way that it did.

Although the incident of Lord North chancing upon the spring may, in itself, seem "trivial" enough, the effect of his Lordship's favourable reports on the medicinal properties of the waters certainly were not trivial, and the result was, in effect, the birth of Tunbridge Wells. In Lord

North's own words: "The use of Tunbridge and Epsam waters, for health and cure, I first made known to London, and the Kings people; the Spaw (*Spa, in Belgium*) is a chargeable and inconvenient journey to sick bodies, besides the money it carries out of the Kingdome, and inconvenience to Religion".

Lord North could have had no idea that, in chancing upon this chalybeate spring, he was, in reality, founding a town with a population of over 40,000, let alone giving a spa name to a Borough of more than 100,000 souls. As Benge Burr himself puts the situation, "There are no corroborating circumstances to be produced from history, or antique monuments", to confirm the traditional date of 1606 for Lord North's "discovery". Nevertheless, Benge Burr does go to some lengths to explain the 1606 date. This he does partly by reference to old manuscripts which mention the fourth year of the reign of King James I. Partly too, he draws upon verbal information obtained by one of his own family from the grandchildren of Mrs Humphreys, the water dipper from whom Lord North is said to have borrowed the vessel from which he first tasted the water. According to one Matthew Benge, Mrs Humphreys was at the time aged 30, some five years older than Lord North, but she lived to the great age of 102.

*Margin note: * * The use of *Tunbridge* and *Epsam* waters, for health and cure, I first made known to *London*, and the Kings people; the *Spaw* is a chargeable and inconvenient journey to sick bodies, besides the mony it carries out of the Kingdome, and inconvenience to Religion. Much more I could say, but I rather hint than handle; rather open a door to a large prospect than give it.

Margin note in Lord North's 'A Forest of Vanities' (1645).

Benge Burr's own background was the book trade, and his History of Tunbridge Wells attracted an impressive list of subscribers, headed by a generous sprinkling from the aristocracy. These included the Earl of Cardigan, FRS, FSA; and Lord Abergavenny, the four times great grandson of the Lord Bergavenny on whose estate Lord North had been staying at the time of his chancing upon the chalybeate spring. The Bishop of London was a subscriber too, as was Samuel Derrick, sometime Master of Ceremonies at Tunbridge Wells. Local worthies who subscribed included Thomas Panuwell and Frederick Pigou, and the work could be purchased locally from Post-Master Edmund Baker's bookselling business in Tunbridge Wells. In London, the work could be brought from Mileson Hingeston in the Strand outside Temple Bar; from the well-known bookseller James Dodsley in Pall Mall; and from Thomas Caslon, sometime Master of the Stationers Company, at Stationers' Court.

Benge Burr's mentor in the book trade was George Hawkins, Bookseller to the Prince of Wales, and Treasurer of the Stationers' Company from

1776-80. Hawkins operated from premises in Fleet Street, but had a shop on The Pantiles during the season in the 1730s and 40s. Papers relating to this, and bills for carriage of goods to and from Tunbridge Wells, by one Edmund Dennes, are preserved at Stationers' Hall[4].

In 1975 the late Alan Savidge, in his book "Royal Tunbridge Wells", drew attention to a little-known paper in the Camden Miscellanies, which indicated a date for the discovery that would have been some nine or ten years later. However, as Alan Savidge pointed out, both that date and the traditional one of 1606 are based, to various extents, on recollections[5].

Importantly though, seventeenth century documentation exists, which can be seen as supporting the traditional 1606 date, in the form of a Petition by local inhabitants to the House of Lords on 16th May 1660.

In the Petition, it is stated that "The wells called Tunbridge Wells have been much frequented *for fifty years and upwards* by many of the nobility, gentry and others."[6]. Thus it seems clear that the Wells had been attracting serious interest among the nobility for a few years before 1610.

During those "fifty years and upwards" before 1660, much activity took place in Tunbridge Wells although not much in the way of building. Lord Abergavenny obtained leave from the Manor of Rusthall to lay a stone pavement around the Spring and to provide in the year 1608, according to Benge Burr, a triangular enclosure of wooden rails.

By 1619, the letter-writer John Chamberlain (1553-1627) was observing:

'The waters at Tunbridge for these three or four years have been much frequented, especially this summer by many great persons, in so much that they which have seen both, say that it is not inferior to the Spa for good company, numbers and other appurtenances'.[7] Chamberlain's remarks seem further to diminish whatever credibility the Camden Miscellanies date of 1615 or 1616 may be thought to have had. If 1616 had indeed been the date of 'discovery', as distinct from the traditional date of 1606, then Chamberlain could not have been referring in 1619 to 'good numbers and appurtenances' at the Wells four years previously, that is to say in 1615. And if 1615 had been the date of 'discovery', the Wells would have had to have acquired fame at such an uncanny speed as to appear unlikely.

Unfortunately, Chamberlain does not tell us who 'the many great persons' were; where they stayed in such numbers; or the nature of the 'appurtenances'. What we do know for certain is that the first royal visitor arrived in August 1629 in the person of Queen Henrietta Maria, the young French wife of King Charles I. Born in 1609, she was said to have a beautiful complexion, large black eyes that sparkled like stars, fine teeth, delicacy of features and an 'air spirituelle'. Henrietta Maria had earlier patronised the thermal springs at Bourbon l'Archambault in France and the waters at Wellingborough in England but, sadly, in 1629 she had just lost her first baby.

Queen Henrietta Maria.

It has been suggested[8] that the Queen's decision to recuperate at Tunbridge Wells, rather than at the more distant Wellingborough, may have been influenced not only by her medical adviser, but also by courtiers such as her Chamberlain, the Earl of Dorset, a Sackville of Knole; Lord Bergavenny of Eridge, a Groom of the Bedchamber; and the Earl of Clanricarde of Somerhill, whose wife was a Lady-in-Waiting to the Queen. Be that as it may, the simple life and waters at the Wells seemed to prove beneficial, and the birth of a baby, who was to be King Charles II, followed in May 1630.

Without the luxury of permanent buildings available near the Spring at that time, the Royal entourage camped in tents on The Common at Bishops Down.

Following Queen Henrietta's six-week long visit, Dr Lodwick Rowzee, a physician from Ashford, published, in 1632, a serious work on the medicinal qualities of the springs entitled "The Queens Welles. That is, A Treatise of the nature and virtues of Tunbridge Water" which gave the medical stamp of approval to the Wells, to such an extent that it was republished several times later in the century.

In this,Dr Rowzee dealt not only with the medical ailments that could be successfully treated with Tunbridge Water, but he also set out guidelines for the quantity of water that should be drunk, and the manner of taking the waters. A "body of competent years and strength" he advised, should begin with 30-50 oz (2½ pints, or about 5 cups) a day, increasing to two, or even four, times that amount; declining, again by degrees, when preparing to leave The Wells. After every few glasses he recommends the taking of some caraway comfits, to help the digestion and the passage of water[9] or, as the 17th century traveller Narcissus Luttrell put it, "to correct the flatulency thereof"[10].

The ladies had the benefit of a "Coffee House" near the springs or, in Luttrell's words: "a conveniency or passing houses when their waters work in a house at ye end of ye walk by ye well".[11] This seems to have been in the vicinity of the present Pink Alley, and to have survived until 1842. For the menfolk, there was the "Pipe-Office" where gentlemen could meet "to converse over a pipe, and a dish of coffee, when they had drank their proper quantity of water"[12]. That, it seems, was probably located in the vicinity of the present Corn Exchange building.

THE
QUEENS
VVELLES.
THAT IS,
A Treatise of the nature and vertues of *Tunbridge* Water.

TOGETHER,
With an enumeration of the chiefest diseases, which it is good for, and against which it may be used, and the manner and order of taking it.

BY
LODWICK ROWZEE, Dr. of Physick, practising at *Ashford* in *Kent*.

LONDON,
Imprinted by *Gartrude Dawson*. 1656.

Title page of 'The Queens Welles'.

Dr Rowzee strongly advocated "betimes" in the morning as the best time of day to take the waters, and by that he meant an hour or so after sunrise. He also recommended that "after you have taken your full quantity, it will do well to walk and stir up and down, and to compose yourself to mirth with the rest of the company; for those who look to reap benefit by Tunbridge, must turn away all cares and melancholy"[13]. Thus "The Walks" adjoining the spring, which we now call "The Pantiles" formed an essential element in the whole Tunbridge Wells modus operandi. It is thought that the Upper Walk of The Pantiles was raised and levelled in the 1630s, and a double row of trees planted to afford shade for the company and tradesmen offering goods.

As the title of his treatise indicated, Dr Rowzee favoured the name "Queen Maries Wells" as "it pleased our gracious Queen Marie to grace this Water by her presence two years ago[14]. However the name did not survive the Civil War and the House of Lords document of 1660 mentioned earlier, is clear about "the wells called Tunbridge Wells".

Henrietta Maria's visit in 1629 not only put the mark of fashionable approval on the Wells, but also gave the waters something of a reputation from a gynaecological point-of-view. During the Civil War and

Protectorate which intervened, Tunbridge Wells understandably saw no royal visitors, but when Charles II was restored to the throne in 1660, post-Restoration Tunbridge Wells became, once again, the most fashionable drinking spa near London. The King himself visited in that year, and again in 1663 with his bride, Catherine of Braganza, an event noted by Pepys in his diary entry for 22nd July.

The Memoirs of the Comte de Gramont describes how in 1663 'the Court left London to spend almost two months in a place than which there is not a more rustic nor a simpler in all Europe but, incidentally, none more agreeable nor more amusing. Tunbridge (sic)... is the rallying-point...of all that is fairest and most gallant in both sexes. The company there is always numerous but always select, and, since those whose motive in visiting it is the quest of amusement always considerably outnumber those who have been brought there by motives of necessity, the whole atmosphere is redolent of distraction and delight. Constraint and formality are banished; intimacy ripens at the first acquaintance; and life led there is generally delicious.'

There followed a series of visits by Charles in 1666 and his brother, James, and his children. James came with his first wife, Anne Hyde, in 1670; and with his second wife, Mary of Modena, in 1674. Princess Anne (later Queen Anne) was several times at the Wells, including visits in 1684 with her husband, Prince George of Denmark, and 1688 and in 1698 with her hydrocephalic son, the young Duke of Gloucester. The child stumbled and fell while playing with other children on the Pantiles. Princess Anne therefore gave money for paving, but was very annoyed to find, on her next visit the following year, that no paving had been laid. Accordingly, she departed abruptly, never to return, although first deputing a superintendent to ensure that the works were properly carried out.

Dr. Rowzee's mix of medical recommendations and 'turning away all cares and melancholy' was the order of the day in Stuart Tunbridge Wells. Nevertheless, as the 17th. century wore on, the search for health was slowly being subordinated to the pursuit of pleasure; and social activities became the prime consideration. The large gathering of people of mixed rank in one place other than the Court, was a novel social phenomenon without precedent. With the pressure of limited accommodation and services came much more informal behaviour among those gathered at the Wells; and the Wells from the 1660s onwards acquired a 'reputation' for somewhat risqué living. An example is this ballad, which appeared in Thomas Rawlin's 'Tunbridge Wells, or A Day's Courtship' performed in 1678:

Imaginary 17th century depiction of socialising at the Wells. Note the large goblet being dispensed on the right of the picture.

BALAD
You ladies who in loose
body'd gown
Forsakes the sneaking City,
And in whole shoals come
trundling down,
Foul, foolish, fair or wity.
Some for the Scurvy, some
the Gout,
And some for Love's disease,
Know that these Wells drive
all ill out,
And cure what e're you please;
They powerfully break the
Stone,
And heal consumptive Lungs;
They'l quicken your conception,
If you can hold your tongues:
Then you that hither
childless come,
Leave your dull Hees behind you,
You'l never wish your selves
at home
Our Youth will be so kind t'you.

The Royal visits drew numbers of notable people to the Wells. However, there continued to be a lack of accommodation near the Spring, and most visitors had to stay in outlying villages or in tents or marquees.

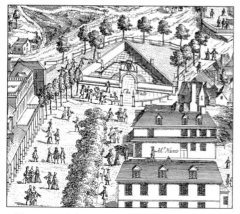

Close-up of the triangular Well setting from Jan Kip's engraving, 1719.

These Royal visits nevertheless stimulated improvements around the Spring itself. The railings were replaced with a stone wall, and there was work to the paving and basins. Flimsy structures on the Walks served as shops and as places of entertainment, until a fire of 1687 afforded an opportunity to lay out the promenade in roughly the form we see today. Columns from the 1690s still survive in the colonnade of No.48 The Pantiles.

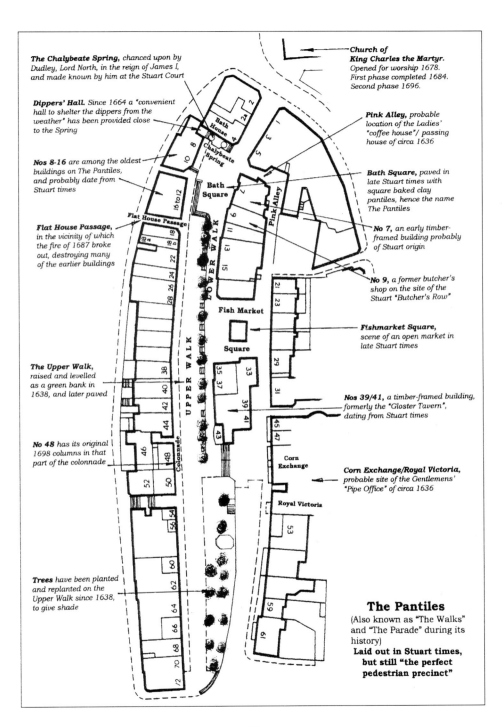

The Chalybeate Spring, chanced upon by Dudley, Lord North, in the reign of James I, and made known by him at the Stuart Court

Dippers' Hall. Since 1664 a "convenient hall to shelter the dippers from the weather" has been provided close to the Spring

Nos 8-16 are among the oldest buildings on The Pantiles, and probably date from Stuart times

Flat House Passage, in the vicinity of which the fire of 1687 broke out, destroying many of the earlier buildings

The Upper Walk, raised and levelled as a green bank in 1638, and later paved

No 48 has its original 1698 columns in that part of the colonnade

Trees have been planted and replanted on the Upper Walk since 1638, to give shade

Church of King Charles the Martyr. Opened for worship 1678. First phase completed 1684. Second phase 1696.

Pink Alley, probable location of the Ladies' "coffee house"/ passing house of circa 1636

Bath Square, paved in late Stuart times with square baked clay pantiles, hence the name The Pantiles

No 7, an early timber-framed building probably of Stuart origin

No 9, a former butcher's shop on the site of the Stuart "Butcher's Row"

Fishmarket Square, scene of an open market in late Stuart times

Nos 39/41, a timber-framed building, formerly the "Gloster Tavern", dating from Stuart times

Corn Exchange/Royal Victoria, probable site of the Gentlemens' "Pipe Office" of circa 1636

Bath House

Chalybeate Spring

Bath Square

Flat House Passage

LOWER WALK

UPPER WALK

Colonnade

Fish Market

Square

Corn Exchange

Royal Victoria

The Pantiles
(Also known as "The Walks" and "The Parade" during its history)
Laid out in Stuart times, but still "the perfect pedestrian precinct"

Between the years 1678 and 1684, Tunbridge Wells' oldest surviving building appeared near the Spring in the form of the delightful church of King Charles the Martyr, with its elegant decorative ceiling by James Wetherell, one of Sir Christopher Wren's principal plasterers.

The Stuart Church of King Charles the Martyr

It was beneath Wetherell's ornate ceiling that John Tillotson (Archbishop of Canterbury 1690-1695) preached before the future Queen Anne in 1688. In the 1690s the church was greatly enlarged and a further decorative ceiling worked by the most celebrated of Wren's plasterers, Henry Doogood. Thus, before the end of the 17th century the once "barren heath" and "wild and unuseful wood" had already given way to some of "the honours" in the words of Benge Burr, "to which Tunbridge Wells has risen."

QUEEN HENRIETTA MARIA
(1609-1669)
WIFE OF KING CHARLES I,
DAUGHTER OF HENRY IV OF FRANCE
Visited Tunbridge Wells 1629

KING CHARLES II (1630-1685)
REIGNED 1660-1685
Visited Tunbridge Wells 1660,
1663 and 1666

KING JAMES II (1663-1701)
REIGNED 1685-1689
Visited Tunbridge Wells 1670,
1674 and 1687

QUEEN CATHERINE OF BRAGANZA
(1638-1705)
WIFE OF KING CHARLES II,
DAUGHTER OF JOHN IV OF PORTUGAL
Visited Tunbridge Wells 1663
and 1666

ANNE HYDE
(1637-1671)
WIFE OF JAMES I WHEN DUKE OF YORK
Visited Tunbridge Wells 1670

QUEEN MARY II
(1662-1694)
REIGNED WITH WILLIAM 1689-1694
Visited Tunbridge Wells 1670

QUEEN ANNE (1665-1714)
REIGNED 1702-1714
Visited Tunbridge Wells 1670,
1684,1688 and 1698

Royal Visitors to Tunbridge Wells from the House of Stuart.

CHAPTER 4

THE RISE OF MOUNT SION

by Philip Whitbourn

"In your return to your lodging" wrote Dr Rowzee in his treatise on Tunbridge Water "I hold it better to ride, than to go afoot".

For early visitors to the Wells, the nearest lodgings were at Rusthall or Southborough, and neither the Manor of Rusthall nor the Manor of South Frith initially saw it as being in their interests to change that situation. However, in the latter part of the 17th century these outlying villages had a rival in Mount Ephraim which lay in Speldhurst Manor. Here a bowling green was enclosed, a tavern opened, lodging houses erected, an assembly room provided, and a pleasure garden laid out. Nevertheless, as Benge Burr tells us "the triumph of this hill was short, Mount Sion became a formidable rival, and quickly eclipsed its growing splendour; for when the bowling green, and the lodging houses arose so near the spring, a less convenient distance was generally avoided."

Benge Burr goes on to observe: "Thus in the course of a few years we find Tonbridge forsaken; Southborough and Rusthall raised and ruined; Mount Ephraim drooping; and Mount Sion in the full bloom of prosperity"[1]. The movement in this direction began in the year 1684, when leases started to be given on South Frith land.

The move seems to have followed the death abroad of Viscount Purbeck, reputedly in a duel, in that year. His widow, Margaret, the heiress of the South Frith lands, was the grand-daughter of the Earl of Clanricarde, builder of the Jacobean mansion at Somerhill. Revelling in dancing and ill-chosen finery, the unconventional Margaret has been nicknamed "The Princess of Babylon", although Tunbridge Wells can be grateful to her and to the soi-disant Lord Purbeck for providing the ground upon which the Church of King Charles the Martyr stands.

Margaret was married three times. Her first husband was Lord Muskerry, who as Lord of the Manor, repaired the Wells in 1664, but he was killed in action soon afterwards in 1665. Lord Purbeck was her second husband, and Robert (Beau) Feilding was her third. Both of these latter men had reputations as gamblers, and, overall, serious inroads were made into Margaret's inheritance. Thus it is not too surprising to find that the early leases for this piece of real estate in the far corner of South Frith Manor were not only in the name of the Right Honourable

24

MAP OF
MOUNT SION
showing the
principal early lodging houses
in solid tone
with some of the other interesting
buildings indicated in outline

now Local Authority (in trust ↓

THE GROVE

formerly Inman's Bush

Grove Villa

(FORMERLY FOOT OF MOUNT SION)

BELGROVE

Belgrove House

The Compasses

P 26~29

Mercer Strip

LITTLE MOUNT SION

was marlborough Ho. ↓

Marlin 2 Strip

LITTLE MOUNT SION

Berkeley Place

BERKELEY ROAD

③

Former Presbyterian Meeting House

FROG LANE

Winefulls Strip

Cecil Court

York House

York Villa

Crescent Lodge 1696

Caxton House

Bricklands (Nash Ho)

Mansfields

HIGH STREET

Blenheim Place and Walmer Cottage

TWITTEN

Sion House

Durnford House *1690 Ho*

MOUNT SION

MOUNT SION

1689

Forest Prospect (Ivy Chimneys)

Jerningham House

1690

Fairlawn House

CHAPEL PLACE

CUMBERLAND GARDENS

Strip?

Howard Lodge

Strip ↑

Eden Ho demolished

Eden Villa *1949*

BEDFORD TERRACE

1834

Church of King Charles the Martyr

Bowling Green

Richmond Villa

Cumberland Villa

Marine House and Cottage

CUMBERLAND WALK

1850's

Caxton House Georgian Brick unlike earlier T/F - Brick houses of 1660+

25

Margaret, Viscount Purbeck, but also that of Sir Thomas Meeres, the principal mortgagee of the Manor lands. The leases are dealt with in some detail by the late Roger Farthing in his excellent book "A History of Mount Sion".

Briefly, the land was divided by the Manor Steward into several strips, together with three less elongated plots of land. In the latter category were the site of the former Bowling Green between Mount Sion and Berkeley Road; the Chapel Block, between Mount Sion, Cumberland Gardens and Cumberland Walk; and a roughly rectangular area around and to the north of the present Grove Villa.

The strips are based upon the two principal roads, namely the High Street and Mount Sion. From the eastern side of the High Street, strips extended in an easterly direction up the slope. The most northerly of these was the Mercer Strip, which included the present Belgrove House and The Compasses public house. To the south of this, the Martin Strip, around Little Mount Sion, included the present Berkeley Place.

Edward Martin, the leaseholder, was one of the craftsmen involved in the construction of King Charles Church. He is recorded as having received the sum of £519-3s-10d for joinery about the Chapel and cupola. Then the southernmost of these High Street Strips was Winefrith's Strip, which had a frontage to Mount Sion itself. In the Sprange engraving on page 32, the Mercer Strip would have been on the left-hand edge of the picture, the Martin Strip in about the middle, and Winefrith's Strip alongside the rising Mount Sion roadway to the right of this.

Off the south side of Mount Sion, sideways strips extended southwards towards Cumberland Walk. These included the Jerningham House Strip and the Fairlawn House Strip.

As a result of these leases a fascinating sequence of former lodging houses can still be seen today by taking a short walk up Mount Sion from its junction with Chapel Place and the High Street.

On the left or north side is Sion House, No.15 Mount Sion, originally built in 1686 by a Mr Powell, just two years after the start of leases being granted. The property continued to be referred to as "Mr Powells" in the Poor Rate throughout Queen Anne's reign, but was known as "Green Pales" in the latter part of the 18th century. By that time, the proprietor of the house was Edward Strange a forebear of E. J. Strange, sometime Mayor of Tunbridge Wells, and C.H. Strange, architect of the Homeopathic Hospital, the pavilion at the Nevill Ground and other local buildings. A

Sion House.

The Twitten, Mount Sion.

Caxton House.

guide of 1780 shows that Green Pales had five parlours and nine chambers. The property has been named Sion House since 1817.

Between Sion House and Caxton House at Nos.19/21 Mount Sion, the picturesque "Twitten" leads to Frog Lane. On the left hand, or western side of the Twitten is tile-hung Crescent Lodge at No.17 Mount Sion and, closing the vista is York Villa.

Caxton House, on the right hand or eastern side, is an Early Georgian building and, unlike the timber-framed Stuart lodging houses, it is brick-built.

Across the road, on the south side of Mount Sion is the large L-shaped form of Jerningham House at Nos.18/20 Mount Sion. Timber-framed and tile-hung, Jerningham House is perhaps the most impressive of the Stuart lodging houses and dates from 1690.

The name of the house appears to commemorate the visits of Lady Jerningham, and her husband Sir William, in the first years of the 19th century. Although Sir William seems ostensibly to have been at the Wells for the benefit of his health, letters written by Lady Jerningham to her daughter Charlotte, later Lady Bedingfeld, provide some interesting insights into the social side of life during "the season". In 1802, we learn that this began on 17th June, when music was played three times a day on The Pantiles, between 9 and 10 am, 1 and 2 pm, and 7 and 8 pm by a harp and several wind instruments.

Jerningham House.

In 1806 Lady Jerningham records in another letter to Charlotte that: "every evening there are meetings at the Rooms or in private houses. And the hours are delightful: Dinner at four, meeting a little after seven, and parting before eleven...". Tonight (1st July 1806), she goes on, "is our first regular Ball. On Thursday there was a hop at the Rooms, begun by your Father and Lady Boyne. He is quite well and in great spirits; this place and the Company of this year particularly suits him".[2]

To the west of Jerningham House, Cumberland Gardens leads southwards past the Regency style Howard Lodge of c.1826 on the left, and the late-Georgian style Bedford Terrace of c.1834 on the right. By the steps down to Cumberland Walk are three houses of special architectural interest, namely Cumberland Villa, Richmond Villa and Marine House. Richmond Villa, No.7 Cumberland Walk, which has a giant Order with ammonite capitals, has been attributed to the Brighton architect Amon Wilds. Marine House at No.8 Cumberland Walk is even more reminiscent of Brighton, faced as it is with beach-like pebbles. Through the 1890s Marine House served as the Vicarage for the nearby Church of King Charles the Martyr.

Cumberland Walk and Mount Sion from Frant Road c.1840.
The tower on the skyline is that of Holy Trinity. To the left of it are the lodging houses of
Mount Ephraim and to the right, the trees of the Grove.

To the east of Jerningham House is Fairlawn House at No.22 Mount Sion. This appears to have started life in 1690 as one of the original Stuart lodging houses, but to have been remodelled in the first half of the 19th century. In 1800 the lodging house offered four parlours, five chambers, five garrets, two coach houses and stabling for twelve horses. A noteworthy occupant in 1828 was John Braham (1777-1856) the English tenor and original male lead in Weber's opera "Oberon". Queen Victoria's mother, the Duchess of Kent was apparently also a visitor to

Fairlawn House, where members of her household are thought to have lodged during the Duchess's stay in 1849 at the now demolished Eden House next door.

Although, sadly, Eden House was lost from Mount Sion in 1969, Eden Villa may still be seen in the view down Eden Road. Numbered 4 Eden Road and dating from 1849/50, Eden Villa was the residence

Balcony at Fairlawn House.

of William Law Pope, the long serving incumbent of the Church of King Charles the Martyr from 1829 until 1877.

At the top of the hill, Mount Sion road turns sharply left around what was once the old Bowling Green. Just before the corner, on the South side of the road, is the house called "Ivy Chimneys", at No.28 Mount Sion. Although now of Georgian appearance, this building also started life as a Stuart lodging house in around 1689/90. In former times the house was called "Forest Prospect", standing as it does at the top of the hill, the property would originally have enjoyed views towards Waterdown Forest to the South and East. Similar views would also have been enjoyed from the Regency style Marlborough House, now Cecil Court, just around the corner.

Returning to the North side of Mount Sion Road, a group of Regency style bow fronts may be seen at nos.23/25 and 27/29 Mount Sion. Nos. 23/25 are at present named Nash House but they were in former times called Bricklands. Also, they were about half their present size when they started life as a Stuart lodging house in the 1690s. However, extension and remodelling took place in Regency times, to give the property its present triple bow-fronted appearance. These probably date from the second decade of the 19th century when the property was in the hands of the spirited local character Richard Delves.

Nash House.

The Delves family loom large in the history of Mount Sion and, indeed, of Tunbridge Wells. Richard Delves' father, Joseph Delves, was at one time in possession of Durnford House at Nos. 27/29 next door. This property, once called Mansfield House, also started life as a timber-framed lodging house of circa 1690. Situated at the corner of Berkeley Road, its East elevation would originally have faced the Bowling Green, which once occupied the flat land in front of Ivy Chimneys.

Turning northwards along Berkeley Road, Berkeley Place stands at the centre of a fork in the highway. Otherwise known as Ashenhurst's Great House, Berkeley Place was built by Thomas Ashenhurst, who also rebuilt several of the shops on The Pantiles after the fire of 1687.

Durnford House.

According to Sprange's guide, Berkeley Place had six parlours and twelve chambers in 1780, and by 1786 the property had become two houses. Visitors to Berkeley Place included the 1st Duke of Gordon (1643-1716), Privy Councillor and Captain of Edinburgh Castle; Sir Charles Cotterell (1654-1710), Commissioner of the Privy Seal; Elizabeth, Lady Onslow, wife of Baron Onslow (1654-1717) Speaker of the House of Commons; and the Duchess of Bolton, wife of the 2nd Duke (1661-1722), Privy Councillor and Lord Chamberlain. During her seven week stay in 1705 the Duchess ran up a bill of £42.10s.

Behind Berkeley Place is Little Mount Sion, from which Belgrove leads to The Grove. Formerly called Inhams Bush, The Grove was originally a wooded area that remained part of the Manor of South Frith until 1703. In that year, John Villiers, the son of Viscount and Viscountess Purbeck, placed the area in trust to be "continually preserved for a Grove and Shade and Walks" for the use of local inhabitants. In doing so, he has, in the words of the late Roger Farthing "bathed in in the gratitude of centuries for his charitable gift." John Villiers liked to call himself the Earl of Buckingham, a title which could have been in order, had the legitimacy of his grandfather been established. The present Buckingham Road defines the eastern end of The Grove. In 1890 control of The Grove passed to the Local Authority, which continues to be responsible for its care.

A view of Mount Sion Hill, Tunbridge Wells, from the Common by J. Sprange in the 1780s.

This view of the Mount Sion area shows Mount Sion on the right, with the L-shaped Jerningham House half-way up it, on the right. At the top, Mount Sion turns to the left into what would have been then, the Bowling Green area. One block to the left of Mount Sion would have been what is now Frog Lane and two blocks Little Mount Sion, curving to the left. The heavily treed area in the background is The Grove.

32

CHAPTER 5

GEORGIAN HIGH NOON

by John Cunningham

While the development of Tunbridge Wells was particularly influenced in the 17th. century by its proximity to London and the Royal patronage of the Stuarts, its development in the 18th.century was influenced by other considerations, such as:

❖ The improvement in access to Tunbridge Wells, through the development of turnpike roads and the stage-coach;
❖ The effect of Bath as a rival; and the relative lack of facilities and accommodation at Tunbridge Wells.
❖ The influence of Richard 'Beau' Nash, as Master of the Ceremonies, who served first Bath from 1705 – 1735 and then both Bath and Tunbridge Wells from 1735 – 1761.

What Tunbridge Wells did not have in the 18th. century was the same degree of Royal patronage as in the 17th century. The Georgian monarchy seems to have avoided visiting the Wells, and this may be due to two considerations – they may have wished to distance themselves from its Stuart associations, particularly since they were threatened by two Stuart attempts, known as the Jacobite 'Rebellions', to regain the throne in 1715 and 1745; and as 'foreigners' in England, they may not have known, or for that matter cared, what was fashionable, since the Georgian monarchy was noted for its somewhat Germanic 'domestic' approach to living.

However while no Georgian monarch ever visited the Wells, their children did, although not all that often. The Prince of Wales (later George II) visited in 1716 and 1724 and his son, Frederick, Prince of Wales, who spent much of his life in opposition to his father, George II, visited in 1739. Frederick was to die relatively young in 1751 at the age of 44, leaving his 13-year-old son as his heir. That son did not succeed to the throne as George III until 1760, when he was only 22. This left for some years a rather large gap in the number of mature, adult royalty available to visit Tunbridge Wells, and in the last two decades of the 18th. century, the inland spas faced new rivals created by the cult of sea-bathing which developed with the Royal patronage of the Prince Regent (later George IV) and his father, George III. The cult had started earlier, but received a significant boost in 1783 when the Prince Regent visited for the first time, Brighthelmstone (or Brighton, as it was subsequently called), and in 1789 when George III began his annual visits to sea-bathe at Weymouth. The cult of sea-bathing was to change the nature of English spas.

From its beginning, Tunbridge Wells was always the closest 'spa' with any reputation, to the capital, London. Of course, there were closer spas – many in what is now London, but which were not then, such as Hampstead, Islington, Kilburn, Sadler's Wells, and Clerkenwell – but they lacked the cachet of Royal endorsement and were probably too close to home to be regarded as having much style, or panache.

The Wells were close enough to travel to, within a day, being between 36 and 52 miles from London, depending on which route you took; and in the 18th. century, there were at least five different, but established, routes.

These five routes may seem a little surprising to the 21st. century reader used to going by the most direct route, but they did recognise that there were other practical/commercial considerations in routing, apart from delivering visitors to and from Tunbridge Wells in the shortest time. Consequently, one route actually went south to Crowborough before swinging west and north to Croydon and London; while another swung wide from Sevenoaks to the east through Otford and Dartford. The five routes listed in Sprange's Tunbridge Wells Guide were:

Table 1 ROUTES BETWEEN TUNBRIDGE WELLS AND LONDON

Via:	Distance in miles
Tunbridge, Sevenoaks, Farnborough, Bromley	36
Tunbridge, Mereworth, Wrotham, Cray, Chislehurst, Eltham, New Cross	40
Sevenoaks, Sundridge, Brastead, Westerham, Godstone, Croydon	50
Crowborough, Maresfield, Nutley, Forest Row, East Grinstead, Godstone, Croydon	52
Sevenoaks, Otford, Shoreham, Eynsford, Farningham, Sutton Street, Darent, Dartford	42

Source: Sprange's Guides to Tunbridge Wells, 1780-1809

Obviously, most visitors would choose to travel by the shortest route, which was the turnpike route, but it is worth noting that there was more than one route to Tunbridge Wells. The most direct 36-mile route could be travelled in less than one day, which was an obvious attraction when more distant 'Spas', such as Bath which was about 100 miles from London, could take 2-3 days.

In the 16th. and 17th. centuries, roads and their maintenance were the responsibility of the parishes through which they passed; and the cost was an unpopular one. With increasing traffic, and with maintenance not always keeping up with wear, there was deterioration in the quality of roads and much dissatisfaction with the speed and comfort of travel. So a solution was devised in the second half of the 17th. century, the turnpike road which was a privately-built higher-quality road for which users had to pay a toll, or fee. The turnpike itself was initially a swinging barrier with 'pikes', or spikes, on the top, to deter people or horses jumping over without paying; and later it became a gate, but the purpose of barrier or gate was to prevent access until the toll was paid.

To build a turnpike road required an Act of Parliament authorising a Turnpike Trust to be set up to build it. In all, between 1663 and 1836, there were 942 Turnpike Acts of Parliament, of which almost half (423) occurred in the 'boom' years of 1751-1775. At its peak, almost 20% of all Acts of Parliament were Turnpike Acts. The cost of building the turnpikes was largely met by local capital, particularly from those who owned the land over which the road ran.

Turnpikes were both a response to growing traffic pressures and at the same time a stimulus to economic growth. The growth of turnpike roads was at first slow, but it later developed into a flood. The first Turnpike Trust was established in 1663, but it took 33 years for the second to follow. Thereafter, the pace quickened. Bath became the 11th. Turnpike Trust in 1708 and the Tunbridge Wells-Sevenoaks Turnpike the 15th. in 1710, and incidentally the first in Kent, clearly indicating the importance of Tunbridge Wells by that time.

By 1730, nearly 60% of the 1,560 route-miles of the 13 main roads into London had been turnpiked; by 1750, the figure had risen to nearly 90%. For the county of Kent, progress was slower. 1761-1770 saw the peak with 281 miles turnpiked, which was over half the total to that date. Previous decades had been much lower:

Table 2 MILEAGE TURNPIKED IN KENT – BY DECADE

	Mileage		Mileage
Up to 1720	32		
1721 - 1730	40	Up to 1750	185
1731 - 1740	25	1751 - 1770	329
1741 - 1750	18		514
1751 - 1760	48		
1761 - 1770	281		
Total	514		

Source: Eric Pawson: Turnpike Roads of 18th. Century Britain

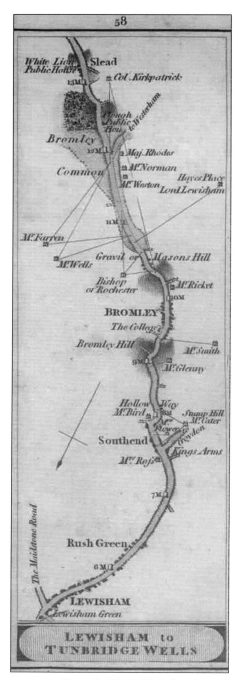

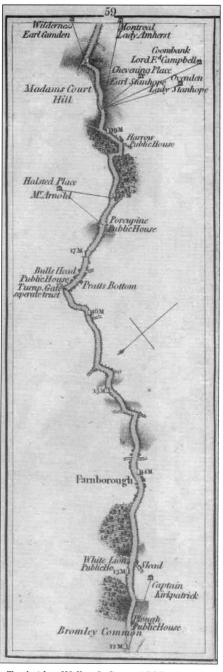

Turnpike Route Map from Lewisham to Tunbridge Wells. J. Cary, 1806.

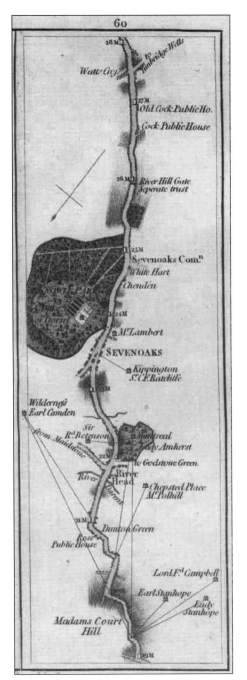
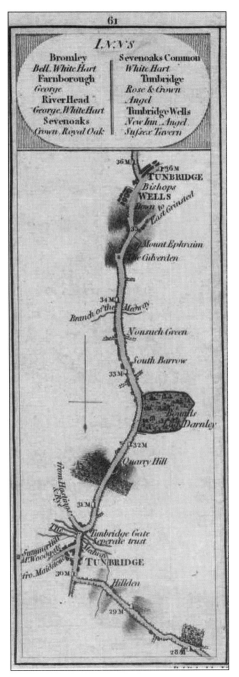

Inns along the route.

Turnpike roads were generally not run for their whole distance by the same Trust, but shared the route with other Trusts, as this table shows:

Table 3 NO. OF TRUSTS AND TOLLGATES INVOLVED IN JOURNEYS FROM LONDON

Route	Date of First Trust	Mileage	No. of Trusts	No. of Tollgates	No. of payments
London to:					
Tunbridge Wells	1710	35	4	5	4
East Grinstead	1731	29	1	4	1
Maidstone	1765	35	2	6	2

Source: Eric Pawson: Turnpike Roads of 18th. Century Britain

The development of stage-coaches – a coach which carried paying passengers on a regular route and with a regular timetable, normally daily – followed that of the turnpike road. The stage-coach first appeared in the 1640's, not surprisingly in London. The wealthy already had their own private coaches and men of all classes (and some women, such as Celia Fiennes) could always ride a horse, but there was a gap in the market – which was particularly for women and children below the private coach level, for whom there was no comfortable or satisfactory means of travel until the arrival of the stage-coach.

Stage-coaches which initially were copies of the private coach, were soon 'improved' in carrying capacity to produce more revenue, and were also improved in design and comfort (particularly in the coach's suspension) for customer satisfaction, in parallel with the development of the turnpike road. The early stage coaches only carried six people, but this increased soon to eight inside, with another six to eight outside and on top. Stage coach suspension also improved and with the improvement in road surfaces and bridges, pioneered by John Metcalf (1717-1810), Thomas Telford (1757-1834) and John McAdam (1756-1836) of tarmacadam fame, road speeds increased, *reaching as much as 10 mph.*

So access to Tunbridge Wells improved and there was a daily (except for Sundays) stage coach to London, leaving at 6 a.m. and arriving at the Golden Cross Inn at Charing Cross in London about 2pm. The return journey left Charing Cross at 6 a.m. the following day and arrived at Tunbridge Wells about 2pm – about 8 hours for a 36 mile journey, an average of about 4½ mph, including probably three changes of horses, two of which may have taken only half-an-hour each, but the third was probably an hour to allow passengers to have a meal. So the average speed on the road would have been about 6 mph.

The single-fare from London to Tunbridge Wells remained fairly static for over a century. In 1697, Celia Fiennes stated that it was 8/- (40p., but worth about £28 at 2005 values) and in 1780 it had risen to only 9/- (45p., but worth only about £24 at 2005 values, because of 18th. century inflation), with outside passengers and children on laps paying half, and the luggage allowance was 14lbs.

Bath (Aquae Sulis) has existed since Roman times as a 'hot-springs' or 'bathing' spa. While the 'bathing' aspect declined as the Roman Empire declined, Bath remained an urban development and the 'hot-springs' became a healing 'holy well' for the sick. In the Middle Ages, Bath was a small but walled city, of about 25 acres, with six gates and a perimeter of less than a mile, enclosing a major Abbey, 300 houses and about 1,000 – 1,500 people. It was a sufficiently prosperous market town for Geoffrey Chaucer to feature the 'Wife of Bath' as one of his 22 Canterbury Tales.

With the Reformation, and the Dissolution of the Monasteries, in the 16th. century, Bath was reduced to being a cloth-making and market town, but the tradition of the sick coming to bathe in the healing waters survived and the Town Council, which now owned the (previously monastic) baths, was not slow to promote their healing qualities. So in the latter half of the 16th. century, Bath enjoyed considerable success, helped by the first of the pseudo-medical tracts to justify the therapeutic qualities of the baths/springs, written by Dr. William Turner and published first in 1569, and endorsed by the first Royal visit in 1574, by Elizabeth I.

So what is surprising is that the established' 'spa' of Bath with an infrastructure of inns and lodging houses, could be challenged and successfully challenged, for a short time in the second half of the 17th. century, by the Wells at Tunbridge, which initially (and for maybe the first 50-60 years) had totally inadequate lodging facilities for its visitors.

The reason was that the Wells at Tunbridge had (short-term) advantages which overrode the already-existing appeal of Bath:

❖   The Wells were very much nearer to London and the quality of the roads, the means of transport and the length of the journey were significant factors.

❖   For a number of reasons, the Wells received Royal approval, which made them not only socially-acceptable, but also socially-desirable.

❖   In the second half of the 17th century, the 'medical' emphasis was on drinking rather than bathing. Probably, for Tunbridge Wells as a drinking spa, the relative unpleasantness of the chalybeate waters was proof of their effectiveness; and drinking water, however unpleasant, is more pleasant than having to bathe in it, (particularly if the water is cold, as it was in Tunbridge Wells.)

So, it was, that the Wells at Tunbridge became the most fashionable 'spa' in the latter 40 years of the 17th. century. But in the long-run, Bath won out and from relatively early in the 18th. century, it took the lead again.

- ❖ The improvements which benefited Tunbridge Wells in the 18th. century – turnpike roads, stage-coaches – also benefited Bath and journeys became shorter. By 1743, all 107 miles between London and Bath had been turnpiked.
- ❖ Bath was already an established town with increasingly fine architecture as the 18th century progressed, while Tunbridge Wells remained little more than a village, albeit fashionable but seasonal;
- ❖ Bath had always had a much larger infrastructure of accommodation and lodging houses, which Tunbridge Wells was never able to match.
- ❖ Bath became a 'drinking' as well as a 'bathing' spa after 1700, and this no doubt also helped it to regain the position it had lost to Tunbridge Wells. (Ironically at much the same time, Tunbridge Wells sought to become a 'bathing' as well as a 'drinking' spa with Cold Baths adjoining the Common and at Adam's Well near Langton Green, but with little success.)
- ❖ In the later 18th. century, Bath was able to develop a Winter Season, made possible by its sheltered position, mild climate and proximity to the newly-developed Mendip coalfields.

And yet, by today's standards, the number of those who attended Bath in an 18th century Season was relatively small and never more than about 12,000. Those who attended the other inland resorts were even fewer. Tunbridge Wells probably had only about 3-4,000 – a quarter/third of Bath's attendance. Tunbridge Wells was surprisingly under-developed in relation to its potential demand. Initially, in the first half of the 17th. century, visitors stayed in a few existing local houses in Rusthall or Southborough or even Tonbridge; and in the early days, even camped in tents on what is now Tunbridge Wells Common. Slightly later, lodging houses started to be built in Rusthall, and on Mount Ephraim. But what is surprising is that they were not built nearer the Wells for the convenience of visitors.

There would seem initially to have been a reluctance on the part of the Somerhill estate which owned Mount Sion and Lord Bergavenny who owned the adjoining land to the south, to allow development on Mount Sion, or south of the Pantiles, or more specifically the Wells.

And so it was Rusthall Manor, which owned the northern part of the Pantiles, the Common, Rusthall and Mount Ephraim, which took the initiative and the rest only followed when they had clear evidence that they were missing an opportunity. Mount Sion started to be developed in 1684, when following the death of Lord Purbeck in a duel abroad, his widow allowed the development of Mount Sion in effect to pay for his debts; and it was to become the fashionable lodging area, displacing Mount Ephraim, Rusthall and Southborough, almost certainly because it was nearest to the Wells.

The other major landowner, Lord Bergavenny, did develop the southern side of the Pantiles (the buildings on the Lower Walks), but it is somewhat surprising that the other adjacent land to the Pantiles which he owned, which became subsequently his Home Farm estate, and which was within 100 yards of the Pantiles, was not developed until the 1890s.

The relative lack of accommodation in Tunbridge Wells, even in the late 18th. century, is well illustrated by an appendix of lodging houses in Sprange's annual Guide to Tunbridge Wells. These can be summarised by area, location and proximity to the Wells:

Table 4 LODGING HOUSES IN 18th.CENTURY TUNBRIDGE WELLS

AREA	LOCATION	No. of Lodging Houses	No. of Parlours	No. of Chambers	Stabling for Horses
Bishop's Down	Bishop's Down	3}3	9	13	23
Mount Ephraim	Mount Ephraim	12}	36	55	100
	London Road	11}23	32	50	69
Mount Pleasant	Mount Pleasant	2}2	8	13	36
Mount Sion	Mount Sion	9}	33	55	57
	Top of Mt. Sion	12}	37	72	91
	Mt. Sion facing Mt. Ephraim	2}	5	11	13
	Foot of Mt. Sion	15}38	44	60	61
Pantiles	Near the Walks	2}	11	18	20
	On the Walks	2}	5	11	–
	Opposite the Walks	11}	22	46	25
	Upper end of Walks	1}	1	2	4
	Nr. Upper end of Walks	1}17	2	3	6
TOTALS		83}83	245	409	505

Source: The Tunbridge Wells Guide 1785 (Jasper Sprange)

41

Parlours were for day-time use and Chambers for sleeping. A Set was normally a Parlour and a Chamber, but a Set could have more than one Chamber to accommodate a family or party, or a spare Chamber could be let separately. Assuming no more than two people to a Chamber, it would seem that Tunbridge Wells even in the late 18th. century could not accommodate more than about 800 visitors at a time. Of course, there may have been further visitors staying with friends in the locality, but these are unlikely to have been numerous. As visitors often stayed for a month, two months and a few even for the Season, one can see why Tunbridge Wells may not have had more than 3-4,000 visitors in a Season. The Tunbridge Wells Season was truly seasonal – it lasted technically from April to October, but the shoulders at the beginning and the end were fairly steep in increase/decline of visitors; and the effective high season was only May-August, a mere four months.

Lodgings were normally taken without board. Most visitors bought and prepared their own food. By 1673, there was a Friday market on the Lower Walk for corn and provisions and by 1686, Lord Bergavenny had been allowed to convert the weekly market into a daily one for provisions, with a monthly cattle market and a fair on St. James' Day (25th July).

By the end of the 18th. century, Mount Sion had become the main lodging area, with just under half of all lodging houses; followed by Mount Ephraim with just under a third; and the Pantiles area with about a fifth.

It is interesting to find that the 83 lodging houses with 409 chambers (an average of only about 5 chambers each) nonetheless had between them, stabling for 505 horses, which would have been essentially for the visitors' own horses. The upper classes would have arrived on horseback, or in their own carriages pulled in a two- or four-horse rig, or in the case of 'Beau' Nash in a coach *and six*; and proper stabling for horses was as important in those days as proper accommodation for visitors.

Tunbridge Wells at that time was busier than its situation might suggest. It was just off the main road from Rye and Hastings to London (now the A21), which supplied the London market with fish. Both Celia Fiennes and Daniel Defoe (who plagiarised her) reported that as many as 300 pack-horses carrying fish passed through Tunbridge Wells each day. This should not be taken too literally as passing up today's London Road, but it would certainly have been within about a mile, through Pembury, which was on the original A21. They also reported that fresh mackerel arrived in Tunbridge Wells from Hastings within three hours of their being caught. (This is probably a slight exaggeration, even by today's speeds.)

To Richard 'Beau' Nash must be given the accolade of ordering and civilising the behaviour of visitors to the Wells. Jasper Sprange, only a few years after Nash's death in 1761 at the age of 87, published this fulsome tribute, cribbing it from Benge Burr's History of Tunbridge Wells (1766):

"Tunbridge Wells, in common with Bath, owes the present agreeable and judicious regularity of its amusements, to the skilful assiduity of the celebrated Mr. Nash, who first taught the people of fashion how to buy their pleasures, and to procure that ease and felicity they sought for, without diminishing the happiness of others."

Richard 'Beau' Nash.

"Before that famous arbitrator of pleasure arose to plan and improve the amusements of the great, public places but little esteemed in themselves, were only resorted to by invalids, to whom their medicinal waters were necessary, and, as the manners of that age were far removed from that easy politeness and refinement of behaviour which distinguishes the present, the company was generally disunited and unsocial, consequently the pleasures to be found amongst them were neither elegant nor diverting. This was the situation of things when Nash made his first appearance at Bath, since which, public places have arose to a great degree of eminence in the fashionable world, and Tunbridge Wells, among the rest, has, from that period, become the general rendezvous of gaiety and politeness during the summer." A bit of an overstatement of both before and after, but nonetheless credit should be given where credit is due.

Richard Nash was born on 18th. October, 1674 in Swansea, South Wales, the son of a burgess, or freeman, of Swansea, by virtue of being a partner in a glassworks. He was educated at the Queen Elizabeth's Free Grammar School in Camarthen; and then at Jesus College, Oxford where he started to read law but left within a year 'probably to escape a woman'. His father then bought him a commission in the Guards, which was equally short-lived, and then entered him at the Inner Temple, where he was more successful, not so much at law but in society. He first showed his genius for showmanship in 1695 when he organised a pageant for William III, for which the King reputedly offered him a knighthood, which he refused since he said that he would need a pension (from the King) to support such a dignity; and such a pension was not forthcoming. He sought his fortunes at the gaming tables without significant success and eventually made his way to Bath in 1704, when he was 30. Here he made a friend of Captain Webster, the Master of the Ceremonies, and when Webster was killed in a duel in 1705, the Bath Corporation were persuaded to appoint him Master of the Ceremonies, without a salary but with a share of the 'perquisites'.

Nash transformed Bath society in a short time. He introduced rules which governed the formality, the style and the ceremony of social life and he introduced subscriptions paid in advance for the financing of the social activities. Swords were banished and dancing was regulated; amenities were improved with a new theatre, a new pavilion, a new Assembly Room and a Pump Room; lodgings and charges were regulated, streets were lit and roads improved. All this encouraged others to take a positive approach to the development of Bath and men of vision, such as Ralph Allen and the Woods, began to build the Georgian city we all admire so much today.

Nash was not to gain control of Tunbridge Wells until 1735, although he made his first visit in 1721 and visited frequently in-between. The reason for this was that Tunbridge Wells had not appointed a Master of the Ceremonies, but there was a person 'in charge' – a 'fine but very large woman' called Bell Causey – who controlled the scene with less formality and less autocracy. Mrs. Causey above all controlled the gaming room for which she was paid two guineas a day (about £150 a day at 2005 values). Not until her death in 1735 could Nash move in, but he did so with speed, declaring himself to be the Master of the Ceremonies.

By today's standards, Nash was many things – an impresario, certainly; a 'gentleman of fortune', probably; a mixture of philanthropist, philanderer and poseur, paradoxically; an adventurer certainly, even a con-man, possibly; and maybe he would have ended up in prison in the 21st century. But he clearly had great style, charm and determination, and he brought system and discipline to what was otherwise a somewhat-disorganised melée. He earned his living by taking a cut – a commission – on all activities, but this did not prevent him from dying poor. In simple Hogarthian terms, he was a Rake, but a very shrewd one who succeeded, or got off lightly (depending on one's view). His Progress fluctuated, but he avoided disaster. He was involved in a variety of scandals but survived – probably the most infamous scandal being over his disputed one-third share in the EO (Evens and Odds) gaming tables at Tunbridge Wells. (EO was a primitive, simplified form of roulette, based on letters rather than numbers, which provided the promoters with a guaranteed return of 2½%, and which was invented by a certain Cook at Tunbridge Wells to avoid the then-current gambling laws, which forbade gambling on numbers.)

Nash's installation in 1735 was followed by the finest season in Tunbridge Wells for many years. Some 900 gentlemen and ladies of quality were there, including (according to Thomas Wilson):

7	Dukes, their duchesses and their daughters
33	Marquesses, Earls and Barons, and their wives, children and relations
16	Knights and their wives etc.
3	Members of Parliament, etc.
3	Colonels, etc.
10	'other persons of social distinction', etc.

And Sir Robert Walpole, the Prime Minister, came down for a few days to see his mistress, Miss Skerrett, who was 'taking the cure'.

While Tunbridge Wells was losing out to Bath during the course of the 18th. century, it was still a fashionable place and there were no signs of it losing 'business'. It was rather that while Tunbridge Wells maintained its numbers, which were essentially limited by the accommodation available, the total market was growing and Tunbridge Wells lost share to the expanding venues of Bath, Harrogate and Cheltenham. But, despite the absence of much royal support, the 'great and the good' still came to Tunbridge Wells. William Pitt – Pitt the Elder, later 1st. Earl of Chatham – and Elisabeth Chudleigh, later the notorious Duchess of Kingston, can be seen, walking with Beau Nash in the Pantiles in 1748, along with Samuel Johnson, in a well-known print by Loggon over the page.

The impact of Nash on Tunbridge Wells was less dramatic than on Bath – he was described by one anonymous pamphleteer as 'King in Bath, but Duke at Tunbridge'. The reasons are fairly obvious – he was at Tunbridge Wells for only 26 rather than 56 years and for the last seventeen years, he was over 70 and inevitably less dynamic; he was also there less often, visiting only in the peak Season, July-August, which fortunately was 'between-Seasons' in Bath. While his visits were relatively infrequent, he

The well-known print of the Pantiles in 1748, by the dwarf-artist Loggon. Dr. Johnson is extreme left, 'Beau' Nash, the Duchess of Kingston and William Pitt centre with their backs to us.

Sarah Porter.

made sure that trusted employees were in place throughout the Season to enforce his 'system'. He brought Sarah Porter – a dragon in the same mould as Bell Causey – from Bath to run the administration. He exuded a combination of style, effrontery and charm, which seems to have succeeded nearly always, but in Tunbridge Wells his rule was not to produce comparable public or private buildings such as he had influenced in Bath. The public room on the Upper Walk was enlarged as an Assembly Room in 1739, but there is little else to show. Part of this may be due to the Rusthall Manor Act of 1739, which is credited with keeping the Wells open to the public and confirming the character and nature of the Pantiles (Parade, Walks), and preserving the Common from any risk of encroachment.

The Code of behaviour which Nash introduced into Tunbridge Wells would already have been familiar to those who had visited Bath. It was based on clear rules supported by a system of subscriptions and dues to fund the services on offer. Sprange published the Rules and Regulations in his 1780's Guide to Tunbridge Wells and these were signed by Richard Tyson, the then Master of the Ceremonies, but they are the same Rules as drawn up by 'Beau' Nash. They are quite short and deserve reproduction in full. It is interesting that to catch attention, the first six Rules start with the relative trivia of the weekly Balls, before turning to the much more fundamental ones to do with supporting financially the infrastructure of Church, the organisers of events, the Dippers, the waiters and the Crossing Sweeper:

RULES AND REGULATIONS
Humbly recommended by the
MASTER of the CEREMONIES
TO THE COMPANY
RESORTING TO TUNBRIDGE-WELLS

I.   That there be Two public Balls every week, on Tuesdays and Fridays. Ladies to pay 2s. *[£5 at 2005 prices]* Gentlemen 3s.6d. *[£8.75 at 2005 prices]*

II. To begin with Minuets, and then Country Dances – All restrictions in point of dress to be abolished, except in regard to those Ladies

---

who intend to dance Minuets, who are requested to be properly drest for that purpose.

III. One Cotillion only, immediately after tea will be danced, and to prevent the time lost in the choice of the particular Cotillion, and in practising it, the Master of the Ceremonies will undertake himself to name it, and its figure shall be previously put up in the Great Rooms, that they may be acquainted with it.

IV. As the custom of dancing two following dances *only*, with the same Lady, at present prevails pretty generally, the Master of the Ceremonies thinks it proper to establish it as a Rule here.

V. The Master of the Ceremonies thinks it almost needless to observe, that it is deemed a point of good breeding, for those Ladies who have gone down with the dance to continue in their places, till the rest have done the same.

VI. The Master of the Ceremonies desires the company to come early, that the Balls may begin at the usual hour of seven.

VII. The Master of the Ceremonies desires to have the honour of presenting himself to the company on their arrival, that he may not be wanting in the necessary attentions to them.

VIII. The Chapel, being originally built by subscription, is not endowed with any provision for an established Minister. – As he depends therefore for his support on the voluntary Contributions of the Company that frequent the place: It is hoped he may rely with confidence for the reward of his labours, on the benevolence of those who reap the benefit of them.

IX. It is humbly requested of all persons who frequent the Rooms to subscribe, to enable the renters of them to defray the many necessary and heavy expences attending them.

X. Besides the Two Rooms, the other general places of Subscription are the Circulating Library, the Ladies Coffee Room, the Gentleman's Coffee Room, and the Post Office.

XI. The Water-dippers at the Spring, who are appointed by the Lord of the Manor, have no allowance, but depend upon what is given them by those who drink the Waters.

XII. The Master of the Ceremonies hopes that it will not be thought improper for him to recommend to families on leaving the place (having been any time there), to consider the Waiters of each of the Rooms. – He will not presume to dictate to public generosity: Those only therefore who wish to be directed in this will receive the necessary information, on application to him.

XIII. It has been an old established custom for every Lady and Gentleman to drop a shilling *[5p.- about £2.50 at current 2005 prices]* into the Sweeper's Box, and as the poor man and his family, constantly attend the Walks, and the Rooms morning and evening, and have no other means of subsisting; it is hoped that none will refuse to comply with so small and equitable a bounty. *(With 3-4,000 visitors a year and assuming two-thirds complied with this 'request', the Sweeper would have received about £5,000 at today's values, but what we do not know is what commission, if any, he had to pay from his 'donations' and to whom)*

The following are the PRICES of CARDS

	£	s	d	
COMMERCE with one pack	0	8	6	Morning 7s.
LOO, one pack 6s. two	0	8	6	
WHIST, two packs	0	8	0	Morning 7s.
PIQUET or ALL FOURS	First pack 5s.			
	Each pack after, 3s.			
QUADRILLE	0	8	6	Morning 7s.
QUINZE ad libitum	0	8	6	
LOTTERY one pack 10, two	0	12	0	

RICHARD TYSON
Master of the Ceremonies

In the context of these Rules, it is also instructive to consider the typical programme followed by visitors. Instead of paraphrasing, let us read the actual words, including some eccentric 18th. century phonetic spelling, of a contemporary, as printed in Sprange's Guide *(which should be read in conjunction with the maps of The Pantiles on page 21 and Mount Sion on page 25)*:

"... your first business is to go to the Well, taste the water, and pay the customary fee, called a welcome penny to the dippers, and at leaving the place you make them a further present, according to the time you have drank waters; you then proceed to the other public places, and there subscribe according to your rank – at the assembly-rooms, a crown *[5/-, or 25p. – about £12.50 at current 2005 prices]*, or more each person; at the coffee-house the same for each gentleman, which entitles him to the use of pens, ink, paper, &c. again, at the bookseller's the subscription is the same, for which you have the use of whatever book you please to read at your lodgings; and here also, is a book open for the ladies. The Library consists of several thousand volumes, of the most entertaining kind; and every new publication is added immediately as published, for the use of subscribers: the newspapers are also taken in daily."

"The band of music likewise, which plays three times a day in the orchestra on the public walks, and at the balls, is supported by subscription, for which a book is open in the great rooms."

"... you may then freely engage in all the amusements of the place. As each of these places depend, for the chief part, on the subscription, is customary for every one in a family to give their respective names to each."

"The company usually appear on the parade between seven and eight o'clock in the morning, to drink the water, and practice the necessary exercise of walking, which is sufficient amusement for an hour or two; they then return to their lodgings to breakfast, or else assemble in parties; and it is customary frequently for the company in general to breakfast together in the public rooms, or at the coffee-rooms; and sometimes in fine weather, under the trees upon the open Walk, attended with music the whole time."

"After breakfast, it is fashionable to attend morning service in the chapel, to take an airing in coaches, or on horseback, to assemble the billiard table, to pass the time in rural walks, to associate in the bookseller's shop, there to collect the harmless satire, or the panegyric of the day, or else to saunter upon the parade; everyone according to his disposition, or the humour which happens to be predominant."

"When prayers are ended, the music, *(which was usually played by musicians positioned in the Gallery still to be seen above no.43)* and which had only ceased during the time of divine service, strikes up afresh, and the company thickening upon the walks, divert themselves with conversations as various as their different ranks and circumstances; so that an attentive listener to the several parties would this moment fancy himself at the Royal-Exchange, and the next at the Palace; now at an India factory, or an American plantation."

"While a great part of the company are thus amusing the time on the parade, others are no less agreeably employed at the milleners, the jewellers, toy-shops, &c. where little rafflings are carried on till the important call of dinner obliges the different parties to disperse." *(The Tunbridge Wells delicacy for which it was noted, was a small bird – the Ortolan or Wheat-Ear, a species of Bunting, which was widely available in the Weald and was said to be 'delicious'.)*

"Dinner finished, the band of music again ascends the orchestra, and you once more behold the company return in crouds to the walk; but now the morning dress is laid aside, and all appear in full and splendid attire, the highest finishings of art and expence being added to the prevailing power of beauty, the insinuation of polite address, and dignity of rank and talents."

50

"In these advantageous circumstances, the general desire of all is to see and be seen, till the hour of tea-drinking, when they assemble together, as in the morning, commonly at the public rooms, or at the coffee-house rooms."

"This over, cards succeed in the great rooms, which are supplied with a proper number of tables, and all necessary accommodations, and where the greatest order and regularity is observed that can consist with the liberty of a public place."

"Twice in a week there are public balls in the Great Assembly Rooms—on Tuesdays at the Room on the Walk, and Fridays at the Lower Rooms; every other night in the week (Sundays excepted, when the company in general meet to drink tea at the Great Room on the Walk) are card-assemblies at each of the public rooms alternately."

"The Master of the Ceremonies has Two Balls in the season, which are generally very brilliant and full. Private Balls too are frequently given by people of fashion in the height of the season; and on these occasions elegant suppers are generally provided."

"Here also are frequent concerts, attended by the most eminent performers in London, where all those who are happy in a taste for music, may be entertained with the most skilful performance, at the expence of a crown. *(about £12.50 at current 2005 prices)*. Sometimes these concerts form a part of the morning amusement under the name of Concert-breakfasts, and then the price of tickets seldom exceeds three shillings and sixpence *[3/6d : 17¹/₂p; about £8.75 at current 2005 prices]*. In these concerts, persons of rank and fortune who have a talent this way, are sometimes admitted amongst the performers, and find a pleasure in joining with the masters in this delightful science."

"Another species of Tunbridge amusement consists in parties to the High Rocks, and other romantic scenes, with which the whole neighbourhood abounds. At these places there frequently are public breakfasts, dinners and tea-drinkings, attended with music, and every incitement to cheerfulness." *(Surprisingly no mention is made of the Race Course on the Common which survived until 1834 and which, together with life in Tunbridge Wells, is satirized in the cartoon on the following page when donkey racing was introduced in 1804.)*

"Excursions to the noblemens and gentlemens seats, the founderies, and many remarkable places in the adjacent country, furnish another pleasurable employment of time at Tunbridge Wells. There are, indeed, several capital houses in the neighbourhood of this place,

Cartoon: Donkey Racing on the Common, 1804.

which, through the polite hospitality of the worthy proprietors, are always open to the inspection of the curious; and there are many pleasant villages, and agreeable prospects in the ways leading to them, that will not fail to attract the distinguishing observer."

"To the article of amusements may I add those of a higher nature, equally calculated for the diversion and improvement of the serious and reflecting part of the company."

"The Circulating Library, and the Coffee House, as mentioned before, are places where the social virtues reign triumphant over prejudice and prepossession. The easy freedom, and chearful gaiety, arising from the nature of a public place, extends its influence over them, and every species of party spirit is intirely stripped of those malignant qualities which render it so destructive of the peace of mankind. Here divines and philosophers, deists and christians, wigs and tories, Scotch and English, debate without anger, dispute with politeness, and judge with candour: while every one has an opportunity to display the excellency of his taste, the depth of his erudition, and the greatness of his capacity, in all kinds of polite literature, and in every branch of human knowledge."

"The bookseller's shop has indeed an advantage over the coffee-house, because there the ladies are admitted; and, like so many living stars, shine in the greatest splendor, while they evidence, that British beauties are no less superior to their sex throughout the world, in the ornaments of the understanding, than they are universally allowed to be in the external graces of the body."

"... the Seasons are now of much longer duration than formerly — some families come as early as March or April, and many continue here till the latter end of November, particularly those who come merely for the benefit of health, the water being reckoned equally in perfection in cold weather, provided it be dry and the air, though sharp, as pure and healthy as in summer."

But nothing stands still and by the end of the 18th century, changing tastes and more competition were the challenges facing Tunbridge Wells and these were to influence the nature and character of Tunbridge Wells in the 19th and 20th centuries:

❖ The rise in the late 18th/early 19th century of the Seaside Resort, inspired by the encouragement of the Prince Regent who visited Brighton from 1783; and by George III who visited Weymouth from 1789.

❖ The development of the Bath Winter Season, which gave Bath an additional edge over Tunbridge Wells.

❖ The impact of the French Revolution, which affected social and economic attitudes for the next 40-60 years, and which in Tunbridge Wells produced 200-300 refugees, who were not there just for the Season.

❖ The impact of the retired Nabobs of the East India Company. These started to arrive in the late 18th century. They were rich, they had not many roots since they had been out of the country for 20-30 years, they wanted to settle, and Tunbridge Wells had many attractions – it was seen as fashionable; it was near to London and the East India Company headquarters; and it was relatively rural, which fitted in with their 'idyll' of what the England of their childhood had been. They, together with the French refugees, became some of the first settlers, rather than tourists, of Tunbridge Wells.

❖ Britain underwent a religious Evangelical Movement – a renewal of personal religion – which started in the mid-18th century with John Wesley (who preached many times in Tunbridge Wells as early as 1762 and as late as 1784) and George Whitefield who was of the persuasion of Selina, Countess of Huntingdon; and which set a strict, pious, serious and unselfish approach to life in an age of low moral standards, which carried through to the 19th century with the Clapham and Oxford movements. This was to be probably the biggest single influence on Tunbridge Wells in the 19th century.

CHAPTER 6

1789 TO 1825 – THE END OF AN ERA?

by Chris Jones

We all know what happened in 1789 – the fall of the Bastille on 14th July and all the subsequent nastiness in France. In the breathless and rather exaggerated description in the *Maidstone Journal* of July 28th: "Paris is a scene of devastation; the streets are covered with dead bodies, many of the Convents are pillaged, and a fourth part of the city is in ashes ... three hundred thousand men are in arms ... from every creek upon the coast, boats are preparing to carry people of property to England."

Against this background the changes that were taking place in Tunbridge Wells were insignificant, but changes there undoubtedly were. If the 17th and 18th centuries at the Wells were characterised by the scandalous behaviour of the visitors; then the two succeeding centuries can equally be represented by the scandalised demeanour of the residents. This 180 degree switch in the mores of the place happened gradually, but three important factors: the loss of fashionable visitors, the growth in the resident population, and changes in the interests and behaviour of the remaining visitors, can all be seen in the period 1789 to 1825. On top of this, the French Revolution and the wars which followed it, affected the Wells as they did the rest of the country.

For the first impact on the Wells we should look at the activities in July 1789, not of the French revolutionaries, but of the English King. For George III, after a long illness, had gone on holiday. But he had not chosen to come to the Wells. He had gone to the seaside, to Weymouth; and he was to return there thirteen times over the next sixteen years. Tunbridge Wells and Bath were no longer the only, or even the most favoured, resorts for holiday or cure. A travel book published early the next century[1] listed nearly seventy watering-places in England and Wales. There were fourteen in Kent and Sussex alone, rivals for the fashionable visitors who had previously brought prosperity to the Wells.

Brighton was the greatest threat to the Wells. It was not the first English seaside resort – there are reports of bathing machines at Scarborough as early as 1735 – but Brighton was easily accessible from the capital, and it had the widest range of facilities. There were lawns where visitors could make their promenade; Assembly Rooms for tea, cards and balls; warm and cold sea baths; the medicated vapour baths of Mr Mahomed, 'shampooing surgeon'; a military band and dashing young officers from regiments quartered nearby; hotels, schools, libraries and banks. There was even a chalybeate spring with water that tasted like that of Tunbridge Wells. By 1821 the town was linked to London by thirty to forty coaches a day. There was even talk of travelling there by balloon – cutting the journey time from London from six to two hours.[2]

Brighton had two particular attractions denied to Tunbridge. First there was the sea. For the adventurous there was sea-bathing, initially recommended as a carefully-regulated medical cure – five minutes before breakfast for healthy males, three dips of two minutes duration three hours after breakfast for females, invalids and children. For everyone else there was the health-giving sea air, and inspirational sea views over

the English Channel. Then there was the Prince of Wales. He first visited Brighton in 1783, and enjoyed the freedom there from the strict Court protocol in London and Windsor. In 1787 he had a farmhouse converted into a neo-classical building which he called his 'Marine Pavilion'. By 1822 it had been transformed into the fantastical Royal Pavilion we know today. Denied worthwhile occupation by his father, he enjoyed instead a fashionable and artistic lifestyle and attracted to himself, and to Brighton, the more flamboyant sections of Society.

The Royal Pavilion, Brighton.

In contrast, Tunbridge Wells seemed tired. According to John Evans, schoolmaster and travel writer, "it is invested by the charms of departed celebrity"[3]. Lord Loughborough, writing in 1786, complained "It has been a great mortification to me to be obliged to pass so much time at Tunbridge, neither amused nor employed ... the place has been altogether uninteresting".[4]

Yet the Wells offered the same facilities and visitor attractions that it had done for years: the Waters, the Common, the Parade with its shops, libraries and coffee-houses, twice-weekly balls and formal occasions for tea-drinking. It was the visitors who had changed. If the more fashionable among Society chose Brighton, then Tunbridge seemed to be attracting those seeking quieter pleasures, and in time it adapted to their preferences. Paul Amsinck, Master of the Ceremonies between 1805 and 1817, contrasted the Wells at the zenith of its prosperity when "the practice of every vice reigned with uninterrupted sway" with

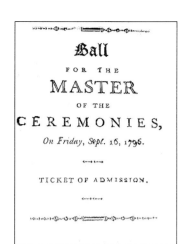

Ball

FOR THE

MASTER

OF THE

C E R E M O N I E S,

On Friday, Sept. 16, 1796.

TICKET OF ADMISSION.

Ball admission ticket.

contemporary behaviour where "the prevailing spirit suggests ease as the criterion of enjoyment: ,,, none are compelled to meet in public, contrary to their inclination".[5] Mary Berry, visiting in 1807, enjoyed the informality that let her walk on the Common at any hour, without hat or gloves, without observation or remark.[6]

John Evans described his own visit. He stayed on the Pantiles, where "melodious sounds rush on the ear with enchanting harmony... It is a grove, or rather an aviary ... so retired is our spot that we can imagine ourselves a hundred miles distant from the metropolis, buried in the recesses of the country."[7] He praised the libraries: "The company ... is select as well as communicative ... Urbanity is at once the sweetener and ornament of cultivated society." There is a 1773 catalogue from one of the libraries preserved in Tunbridge Wells Museum.[8] It includes over a hundred books in French – literature, history, biographies, religion and travel – it was indeed a cultivated society.

The attractions were not all, to use Evans' description of the waters, 'colourless and invariably temperate'. He describes the excitement of an outing to High Rocks. Into the valley 'torrents of rain had fallen, so that deep ruts shook our vehicles. The ladies were in trepidation. But the skilfulness of our rustic juvenile drivers overcame every obstacle" and on reaching the Rocks there were "huge masses of stone thrown up by an earthquake – exhibiting a frowning aspect towards all who approach them".[9] On another occasion, when descending Mount Ephraim, he came across booths containing "the wild beasts of the forest, whose roarings disturbed these haunts of retirement".

To the visitors, the attractions of the Wells might have seemed natural, but in reality the facilities required maintenance, and this fell to the land-owners, landlords and traders. In 1782, the sale of timber from 25 decayed oaks in the Grove enabled fences to be made good and painted, benches to be constructed, a walk to be laid out and the ride repaired.[10] In 1792 the decayed paving of the Upper Walks was replaced by Purbeck Stone, brought by sea to Rochester, then up the Medway to Wateringbury, and from there by cart to the Wells. It cost £710.15s.4d, raised by public subscription.[11]

The Walks were renamed the Parade. Perhaps they thought that sounded grander – the visitors, however, Lady Jerningham and Mary Berry, continued to call them the Pantiles. In 1799, on a somewhat different scale, a minute hand was added to the clock of King Charles the Martyr.[12]

Improvements to the spring were also found to be necessary. By 1789 the old stone basin was badly decayed, and was replaced by a new one in marble, with a cover, to keep contaminants out. The new arrangements, however, were not welcomed by all. Some 'old frequenters of the place' claimed that they no longer benefited from the water in the same way, and they were not persuaded by argument or by chemical analysis. The new cover had to be removed and the complainers were indulged 'with the essence of the dipper's fingers, and the filtration from the accumulated filth beneath'.[13]

Some of the changes went beyond mere maintenance, the construction of the Bath House in 1804 for example. Now one of the iconic buildings of the town, it was an attempt to compete with spa resorts which were able to offer warm and cold baths. It was designed for Mrs Shorey, Lady of the Manor of Rusthall, by the architect John Thomas Groves, who was later to design the Nelson Monument at Portsdown. It provided cold and warm, vapour and shower baths; and

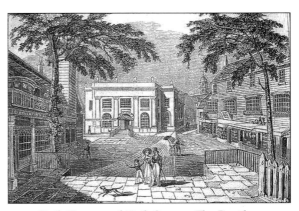

Bath House and Bath Square, The Pantiles.

water from the spring was fed through into a pump room. The spring itself remained outside the building, where it is today, though the canopy over it was not added until later. Apartments were planned on the first floor. In a strangely understated comment in the 1811 edition of his Guide, Sprange says that the Baths "have proved much to the benefit and comfort of those who have had occasion to use them."

Sprange's guidebooks also describe an earlier attempt to attract visitors – the cold bath at Adam's Well. The site was bought in the 1760's by a Mr Pinchbeck, and the water was found to be notable for its purity (it is not chalybeate). He built a 'commodious stone bath' to attract visitors and published numerous testimonials proclaiming its efficacy in the treatment of skin ailments. He also dug an outside bath for the benefit 'of the poor, and for dogs and horses'.[14] Margaret Barton is sceptical, however, of its success, and writes "no visitors, so far as is known, paid the slightest heed".[15]

A more successful venture was the Theatre on the Lower Walks run by Sarah Baker. She set up her first theatre at the Wells in 1786 on Mount

Sion. In 1789, having triumphed over a rival in Castle Street, she moved to the Lower Walks, to the site of the current Corn Exchange. Her theatre there was small but throughout the 1790's and 1800's put on two or three well-attended performances each week during the season. Mrs Baker

The Theatre on the Pantiles, now the Corn Exchange.

died in 1816 and was succeeded by William Dowton, her son-in-law and a nationally-recognised actor-manager.

The Museum includes a wonderful collection of posters, playbills and other ephemera from this period, left by John Sprange, printer. From these we can see that there was horse-racing each year on the Common, cricket matches, fireworks on the Grove and cock-fighting. A poster from 1797, for example, advertises a MAIN of COCKS to be fought by the Gentlemen of West-Kent, against East-Kent, for two guineas a Battle, ten guineas the Main. The fighting began at nine o'clock in the morning.[16] It is possible that the horse-racing in particular was an attempt to copy the attractions of Brighton. The same might also apply to the introduction in 1801 of donkey riding – attributed to Lady Georgina Seymour.

Another significant change was beginning to have an impact – the growing number of permanent residents. Martin Yorke, for example, Major in the East India Company, retired rich from his service in the East and settled on Bishop's Down. Richard Cumberland, noted dramatist and some-time diplomat, moved from London in 1779 to live on Mount Sion. Their presence made a difference to the Society of the Wells, particularly outside the Season, when it had traditionally been deserted. While Cumberland was a celebrity and attracted visitors, it seems that he was, unfortunately, something of a bore. Major Yorke by contrast was "Social in his habits, liberal in his principles, and fervent in his attachments. His house was the constant scene of friendly intercourse and cheerful hospitality; whilst his warm heart diffused throughout his neighbourhood the benefits of active exertion."[17] Once there was this nucleus of permanent residents, it attracted others; and their hospitality drew the seasonal visitors away from the organised public entertainments on the Parade.

Visitors and residents could not isolate themselves completely from the outside world. The Revolutionary and Napoleonic Wars which lasted on and off for nearly twenty-five years had their impact. There was an appeal in 1793 for subscriptions to support twenty-three emigrant priests sheltering at the Wells; and M. Seignoret de Villiers, formerly Captain of Cavalry, advertised Readings in French, claiming to have saved ten English sailors, prisoners alongside him under the tyranny of Robespierre.[18] Rather more exalted refugees – the Prince and Princess of Orange, forced out of the Netherlands when the French invaded in 1794 – stayed for some weeks at Mount Pleasant House.

Arrangements were made for the removal, preservation or even destruction of livestock in case of invasion.[19] Appeals were made for Gentlemen Volunteers and Able-Bodied Men to join the Marines and Navy. Prayers were printed for use on national Days of Fasting "for obtaining Pardon of our Sins and imploring His Blessing and Assistance on His Majesty's Armies and Fleets".[20] Within Tunbridge Wells, Richard Cumberland was active in recruiting and drilling volunteer forces. He was very proud of his four companies of infantry "I had not a private that was not ... soldier like ... for they were all artisans, mechanics, or manufacturers of Tunbridge Ware and I had not one who did the work of a mere labouring peasant".[21] The volunteers were disappointed to be disbanded at the start of the short-lived peace of 1802. None more so than Cumberland himself, who wrote "I have so long regarded you as my

Tunbridge Wells, August 1, 1801.

To all young Men, able and willing to bear Arms in Defence of their Country.

WHEREAS it is probable that the Enemy may rashly attempt a Descent upon the neighbouring Coasts of Kent or Sussex, in which case it is to be presumed your Zeal would prompt you to stand forth in the Defence of every thing that is dear and sacred to you as Englishmen, I give you this Notice that I have Arms, Cloathing, and Accoutrements ready to distribute to such young Men, as shall offer to enroll themselves, and as shall be judged fit and proper to be enrolled in the brave and loyal Corps of Volunteer Infantry, which I have the Honor to Command.

RICHARD CUMBERLAND,
Major Commandant.

Printed by J. Sprange, T. Wells,

Call to Arms, 1801.

friends, my comrades, and I may even say as my children, that I cannot part from you without the most sensible regret".[22] There were benefits from joining the Volunteers – exemption from the tax on hair-powder, for example – worth £1. 1s per year. And Volunteers were exempt from the Militia Ballot. There were other ways of avoiding militia service – Sprange acted as agent for the Western Militia Society, which, for a premium of 16 shillings, would supply a substitute in the event of the policyholder being selected in the ballot.[23]

Of course there were residents and visitors who actually served in the wars. Major Yorke for example, was killed during the 1806 campaign against the Cape of Good Hope – a rather tragic story as the Cape had been captured from the Dutch in 1795, only to be returned to them at the Treaty of Amiens in 1802.

During the war there were occasional events, some religious, some social, to celebrate victories, 'Diversions on the Commons', for example, arranged in 1799 'by the Gentry visitors to promote holyday happiness'. These included stool-ball, a sack race, and a 'jingling match' – which seems to have been a form of reverse 'blind man's bluff'. It is not clear how typical these activities were of Tunbridge Wells – the Gentry visitors may simply have copied them from Tonbridge where they were a feature of the annual hiring fair for farm servants.[24] In 1812 there was a celebration of the victory at Salamanca. We have a record of it from Mary Berry: "In the evening there was a general illumination. The Pantiles were decorated very prettily with branches of ash mixed with flowers and laurels. I had often heard of the beauty of an illumination at Tunbridge but it very much surpassed my expectations. The effect of Mount Sion from the Common, with its rows of houses raised one above another and all lighted would have been beautiful, but for the bonfires which they are in the habit of making [by burning the furze on the Common]. It produces a grand effect of light, but the smoke prevented our seeing the illumination of the village".[25]

The war had other effects. The improved navigation of the Medway meant that it was easy to transport timber down to the naval shipyards at Chatham – to the detriment of the local landscape. Amsinck sought consolation in the thought that the lost oaks were being used "to so noble a purpose ... by their annoyance to our enemies in every quarter of the globe".[26] There was no longer a local iron industry to supply cannon to the war effort, but the local powder mills were presumably busy. And the paper mill near Langton, having been noted for making fine writing paper, was now employed in providing cartridge paper for the Tower of London.

As for other industries there was the manufacture of Tunbridge Ware. This had been sold in 'toy-shops' on the Parade for much of the 18th century though the technique of applying a mosaic veneer was a 19th century development, and may not have been used in our period. Barrow's map of 1808 shows five establishments: Burrows and Co in Jordans Lane (Church Road), Sharp's in Culverden Row, Johnson's and Fenner & Nye's at either end of Bishop's Down, and Fenner's in Mount Sion. We should not, however, over-estimate the size of these concerns. In 1841 there were still only 23 people employed in total.[27]

The following, and all other Articles of

Tunbridge Ware,

Wholesale, Retail, & for Exportation:

New invented Tunbridge Ware Ear Rings
Music Stands, Ornamented, or Plain
Stands for Flowers, with Prints, or Plain
York and other Spinning Wheels, ditto
Tables elegantly Inlaid, ditto
Dressing and Hand Glasses, ditto
Writing Desks of all Sizes, ditto
Ditto Boxes, ditto
Work Baskets and Boxes, ditto
Portable and other Book Shelves
Dressing and Shaving Boxes
Sallad Spoons and Forks
Elegant Card Racks with Prints, or Plain
Card Boxes with Counters, ditto
Cribbage Boards and Trays, ditto
Boxes of various Sizes, fitted complete
    with *Reeves'* and *Newman's* Colors
Tea Caddies and Boxes, with Prints, or
    Plain
Medicine, or Cordial Chests, ditto
Draught, or Backgammon Boards, &c.

Tunbridge Ware advertisement.

Amsinck explains that there wasn't much agriculture around the Wells either – the soil wasn't good, and the leases too short. He also blames the better returns that had been available from smuggling, and he mentions another oddity – the idea that the local water was injurious to horses. This meant that visitors preferred not to bring their own horses, and even the local hackney carriage operators stabled their horses overnight in Southborough.[28] But even so, the select Company at the Wells was closer to rural life than we might expect. One of Sprange's notices threatens those who let their hogs, asses, horses and cows roam through the streets, and he himself kept hens, bees and cows in his garden. In 1796 the sale of thirty waggon-loads of 'exceeding good rot DUNG' was advertised at the White Bear.[29] But when

D U N G,

TO BE SOLD

BY AUCTION,

BY E. STRANGE,

On *Wednesday,* the 2nd day of *March,* 1796,

Between the hours of Two and Four in the Afternoon,

IN ONE LOT,

At the House of Mr. J. CALLOW,

White-Bear, Tunbridge-Wells:

A LARGE quantity of exceeding good ROT DUNG, containing by estimation, Thirty Waggon Load, the property of the said Mr. J. CALLOW.

country-loving William Cobbett made an over-night stay in August 1823 he could not escape quickly enough the 'contagion of its Wen-engenderred inhabitants'.

By the 1820's the change in the interests of the visitors was being reflected in the official programme of events. Between 1808 and 1811 the twice weekly balls (Tuesdays and Fridays) were reduced to Tuesdays only. There is a rather anguished Notice from Richard Tyson (MC 1780-1801) complaining that the Company seems to have ignored the balls altogether: "The usual mode of notification of the Day for the commencement of the Balls not having been so fortunate as to meet with any attention" and he goes on to make the point that the Place was entirely supported by its visitors and would be in an unhappy condition if they were to withdraw their favour.[30] In 1797 the profits from the Season had not been sufficient to provide for the maintenance of the Musicians, and an extra Tea-Drinking event late in the season had to be arranged for their benefit.[31] By 1815 there was no longer reference in the Sprange guide to 'frequent concerts'.

We should be wary of attributing these changes to a reduction in the total number of visitors. In fact there seems to have been an increase in the number of rooms available for visitors.[32] It was rather a change in the preferred activities of the visitors. There is a letter from Sir Charles Pratt to his daughter saying that the assembly rooms are half-empty, and that half of those attending had no male partners, but he continued with the comment that it "is of no consequence to us, who would not mix with the crowd if the place were full".[33] And a rather nice quote from Lady Jerningham that "Tunbridge is like a large Convent, everyone asleep in their beds before twelve" is not the complaint that it first appears. The full sentence begins "The Hours are delightful: Dinner at 4, meeting a Little after seven, and parting before eleven, so that Tunbridge is Like a Large Convent ...". Although she enjoyed the balls, she also enjoyed other more private socialising: "We have not such fine People here this year, but perhaps more Sociability, for there are Meetings every Night in private Houses".[34]

It may be that this move away from the very public form of entertainment that had characterised the Wells was due to the behaviour of some locals. A Notice from Viscount Boyne JP refers to "complaints of Nuisances ... to the great annoyance of the Company". To counter these he appointed four special constables "to prevent any Boys or Girls assembling on the Parade to Play, or in any other manner interrupting the Company ... [especially] on a Sunday evening, which has so shamefully prevailed of late, to the great disgrace of the Place, to the corruption of their morals, the encouragement of vice, and to the weakening of every religious Principle".[35] Amsinck also complained that "the days of decency and good order are gone by". He spoke of the tea-drinking events in earlier decades that were held on the Parade when "there was never any advance on the part of the lower classes to disturb the comfort of the meeting" and contrasts them with the "unmannerly intrusion of the present time".[36]

Tunbridge-W.....March 2d, 1797.

Daring Outrage.

FIVE GUINEAS REWARD,
On Difcovery.

WHEREAS fometime in the Night of Tuefday laft, fome Perfon or Perfons did, by Violence force the Shutter, and get in at the Window of the CARD-Room, belonging to Mifs SPRANGE, on the Parade, and there with evident Malicious Intent, cut and mangle the Outfide of a SEDAN CHAIR, tore away the Top, cut up and entirely deftroyed the Cufhion, took away the Poles, broke them in feveral Pieces and thew them on the Common.

Whoever will difcover the Offender or Offenders, fo that he or they, may be brought to Conviction, fhall receive FIVE GUINEAS Reward.

One of the many examples of anti-social behaviour recorded in the Sprange Collection

There was still the occasional special event. In 1820 there was a ball at the Assembly Rooms arranged by supporters of Queen Caroline, led by the Duke of Sussex, to celebrate the collapse of the divorce case against her. However, while dancing was in progress 'some sturdy members of the opposite faction rushed into the ballroom, hustled the musicians and carried off their instruments'. Undaunted, the dancers elected their own Master of the Ceremonies (the official MC being of the 'opposite faction'), and continued their quadrille without instrumental music, tunes being hummed 'by such of the company as had the talent'.[37]

Such events were exceptional. In 1810 Amsinck was already writing "50 years ago seasons lasted from Midsummer to Michaelmas ... Many houses ... are now permanently tenanted. From a migrating colony ... Tunbridge Wells has become a place of considerable wealth, consequence and respectability".[38] The population figures tell the same story, increasing from about 1000 in 1801 to almost 6000 in 1831. Life was not always comfortable for the new type of visitor. In a letter of December 1813, Lady Wilton wrote "My sister is now at Tunbridge with Miss Harbord, they both complain of the extreme coldness of the Place.... Lodging Houses have thin walls, and are not calculated for comfort in December.'[39]

The changes were to continue after 1825. After the retirement of Lieut. Madden in 1836, no further Master of Ceremonies was elected. By the 1850's the regular season of balls had been discontinued. The Bath

House was converted to a shop in 1847, and the Theatre closed down in 1843. There was excitement in the 1820's and 1830's over the visits of the young Princess Victoria with her mother and half-sister. The town made the most of its new royal patroness. But the world of the young princess, who recorded in her journal that she was in bed by twenty past nine, was a very different one from that of her royal predecessors two centuries earlier.

The following extract from Thackeray's 'Tunbridge Toys' was written beyond our period, in the 1850's, but it works well as an elegy for the life that was the Wells – by then already no more than a memory.

"I wend my way to the Pantiles, the queer little old-world Pantiles, where, a hundred years since, so much good company came to take its pleasure. Is it possible, that in the past century, gentle-folks of the first rank ... assembled here and entertained each other with gaming dancing fiddling and tea? There are fiddlers, harpers, and trumpeters performing at the moment in a weak little old balcony but where is the fine company? Where are the earls, duchesses, bishops and magnificent embroidered gamesters? A half-dozen children and their nurses are listening to the musicians; an old lady or two in a poke bonnet passes; and for the rest, I see but an uninteresting population of native tradesmen."

The Pantiles, c.1840. Was it no more than 'an uninteresting population of native tradesmen'?

CHAPTER 7

CALVERLEY NEW TOWN

By Philip Whitbourn

When J.D.Parry's "Coast of Sussex" was published in 1833, the author extended his account inland to include Tunbridge Wells. "Its site on three hills", he said, "is almost as well known as that of Rome". Mount Sion he described as containing the principal part of the old buildings, apart from The Wells and its walks. Mount Ephraim was credited with a situation commanding the most bracing air in the neighbourhood, and beautiful views. Mount Pleasant, on the other hand, was said to be "inconsiderable". That, however, was already changing.

Some seven years earlier, in 1826, John Ward Esq. of Holwood, Kent, had concluded a series of transactions that enabled him to put together his Calverley Estate. This, as may be seen from the map on p.66 included Mount Pleasant and, north-eastwards, a tract of land extended all the way to Pembury. In total, the estate comprised some 874 acres, 56 acres of which, at the eastern or Mount Pleasant end, he earmarked for building. Thus, when Colbran's guide for Tunbridge Wells was published in 1844 it was able to report that "it was evident that a new town was springing up –villas, a terrace, a parade, rows of shops, etc. soon began to develop themselves, and advanced steadily to completion".[1]

The realisation of this Calverley New Town depended upon three main components.

First, there needed to be an enlightened landowner; secondly, a talented designer; and thirdly, but by no means least, an investor-builder willing

and able to turn a vision into reality. The enlightened landowner, as has been said, was John Ward, sometime Deputy Lieutenant for the County of Kent, High Sheriff, and an M.P. The talented architect for the enterprise was Decimus Burton, Fellow of the Royal Society, Fellow of the Society of Antiquaries, and sometime Vice-President of the Royal Institute of British Architects. Ward and Burton had worked together before. Burton had designed Ward's mansion Holwood at Keston, near Bromley, and the two of them had been involved, together with the architect John Nash

Decimus Burton.

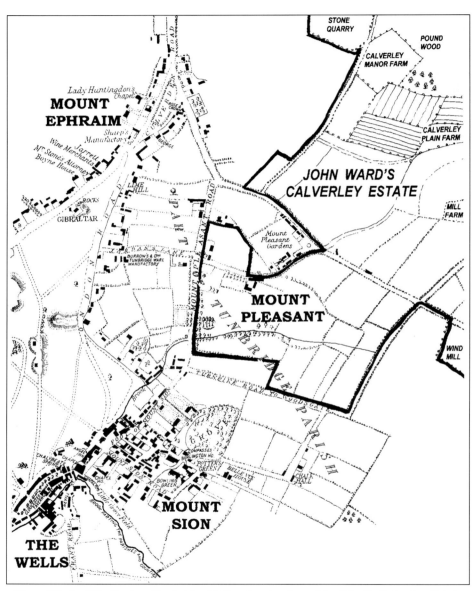

Map of Early 19th Century Tunbridge Wells, showing how John Ward's Calverley Estate extended into the heart of the present Town Centre.

and others, on the pioneering residential park at Regent's Park in London.

Regent's Park was a pioneering project in more ways than one. John Nash, as the overall designer of this early residential park, placed much emphasis on the planting of the sites within the Park. This he saw as important, partly for the scenic effect of the park but also, to screen the villas from each other. The aim, in his mind, was to produce 'an entire park complete with unity of character', as distinct from a development that was simply 'an assemblage of villas and shrubberies.'

The method of realising Nash's Regent's Park scheme could be said to be pioneering too, in that it marked the emergence of the speculative builder to a greater extent than generally been the case up to that time. Although Regent's Park formed part of the Crown Estate, its development was not carried out by the Office of Works, but by private builders relying on private capital. Foremost among those investor-builders involved, was Decimus Burton's father, James Burton.

Although Decimus Burton and John Ward were major players in the realisation of the Regent's Park scheme, they did not occupy the key position of John Nash and James Burton in that enterprise. Ward was unusual in the Regent's Park story, in that he was purely an investor, as distinct from an investor-builder. He had invested in the problematical Regent's Canal project, and he also held leases on Clarence Terraces, together with some other Regent's Park properties built by James Burton, with whom he had close associations.

John Ward and Decimus Burton effectively brought the Regent's Park concept and methodology to Tunbridge Wells. Whereas the Commissioners for Crown Lands had granted building-leases for Regent's Park, John Ward granted them for Calverley Park. And, whereas John Nash co-ordinated design in Regent's Park, Decimus Burton did so in the Calverley development.

The sound investor/builder for the Calverley development, Colbran again confirms, was "Messrs. Bramah of Pimlico, having taken the ground necessary for the purpose, on a building lease".[2] At first sight it may seem somewhat surprising that a firm best known as locksmiths, should appear on the Tunbridge Wells scene to turn the scheme produced on paper by Ward and Burton into an actual New Town. It is true that the Bramah firm was well-known to Decimus Burton, having made the magnificent cast iron gates at the Wellington Arch in London to Burton's design. It is true, also, that the Bramah firm had quite wide interests and experience in various sectors of the building industry.

The firm was founded in the latter part of the 18th century by the versatile engineer and inventor Joseph Bramah (1749-1814), whose diverse interests included water closets, locks and keys, a sawing machine, a planning machine and, importantly in engineering terms, a hydraulic press.

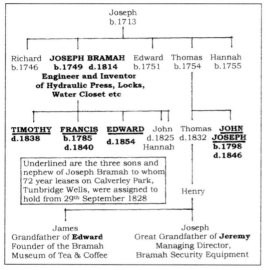

Abbreviated Family Tree of Bramah family.

Joseph and his wife Mary had four sons and a daughter. The eldest son, Timothy, became a partner in the firm in around 1813 (3) and the next two, Francis and Edward, sometime after their father's death in 1814. Joseph's entry in the Dictionary of National Biography states his "Wealth at death" as under £45,000. How much under that figure the DNB does not say, but £45,000 in 1814 would have been worth well over £2 million in today's money. So perhaps by the 1820s, the family may have seen the Tunbridge Wells venture as a potential investment opportunity. Be that as it may, with all the attendant risks of such projects, there is no question about the family's key role in the development of the Calverley New Town. Documentary evidence exists at the Centre for Kentish Studies at Maidstone concerning an agreement between John Ward and the Bramah brothers Timothy, Francis and Edward, together with their cousin John Joseph Bramah, regarding leases on ground in Calverley Park[4]. Bramah's Tunbridge Wells workshops in Camden Road are shown on Britton's 1832 map[5] and, although they have long since disappeared, the building that once housed Bramah's Tunbridge Wells office and counting-house at 6 Calverley Place[6] is still there, re-numbered 67 Calverley Road.

The double-page maps on pages 72-73 shows Decimus Burton's original plan in 1828 for developing the Calverley Estate; together with a modern map on page 74-75 of what was actually developed, which indicates in solid tone those buildings and features that still survive.

Holy Trinity Church and the Priory in 1832.

The earliest of these is Trinity Church, now Trinity Arts Centre, which lies just outside the Ward Estate and pre-dates the rest of the scheme by a year or so. Georgian "Gothick" in style, its first stone was laid in 1827 and the building was opened in 1829. Adjoining Trinity two of the three charming "Gothick" Priory Houses survive, Nos. 2 and 3, The Priory having recently been restored and brought back from office to residential use.

Calverley Parade, demolished in the 1930s to make way for the Civic Centre. The stone wall survives alongside the War Memorial.

69

Across Mount Pleasant from Trinity, the Civic Centre complex now occupies the site of the former Calverley Parade, Calverley Mews, Calverley Mount and most of Calverley Terrace. All that remains of this group now are Nos. 9 and 10 Crescent Road and some stone walling along Mount Pleasant and Crescent Road.

The former Calverley Hotel, currently renamed the Hotel du Vin.
A remodelling by Decimus Burton of the old Calverley House.

Opposite Nos. 9 and 10 Crescent Road, is the Hotel du Vin, formerly the Calverley Hotel, which was opened in 1840 by Mr Edward Churchill.[7] Churchill is recorded as having contributed groceries, preserves, plum puddings, candles and soap to the Crimean Army Fund during the Crimean War of the 1850s.

The Hotel was a remodelling by Decimus Burton in c.1839 of the old Calverley House, where the young Victoria and her mother, the Duchess of Kent, were residing when work on the Calverley New Town started.

Thus the nearby Victoria Lodge entrance to Calverley Park was appropriately named after the Queen. The rooms on either side of the central archway have a Greek Doric Order.

Victoria Lodge, Calverley Park.

The other two lodges, Keston Lodge and Farnborough Lodge are named after the lodges to John Ward's Holwood Estate.

Farnborough Lodge, Calverley Park. In the "Gothick" taste.

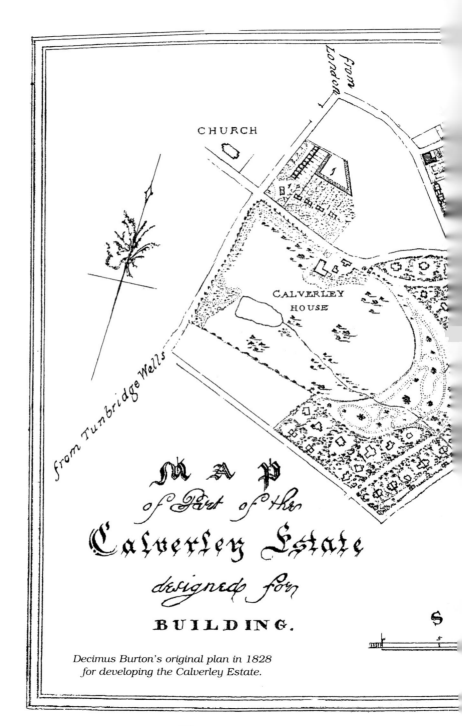

from London

from Tunbridge Wells

CHURCH

CALVERLEY
HOUSE

MAP
of Part of the
Calverley Estate
designed for
BUILDING.

S

Decimus Burton's original plan in 1828
for developing the Calverley Estate.

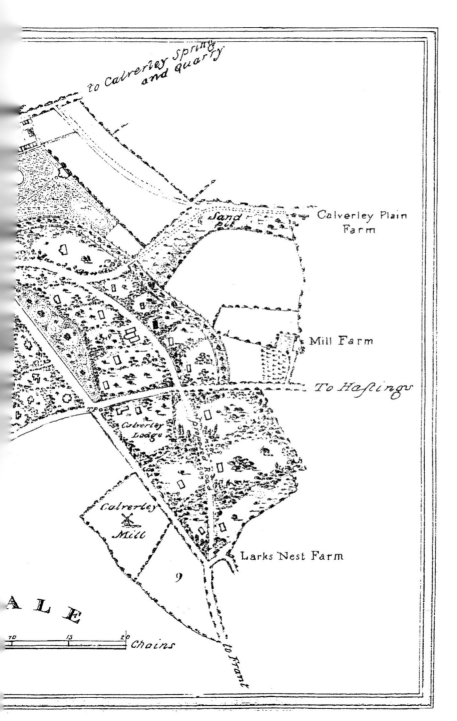

to Calverley Spring
and quarry

Sand
pit

Calverley Plain
Farm

Mill Farm

To Haſtings

Calverley
Lodge

propoſed Road

Calverley
Mill

Larks Nest Farm

9

A L E

10   15   20
Chains

to Frant

73

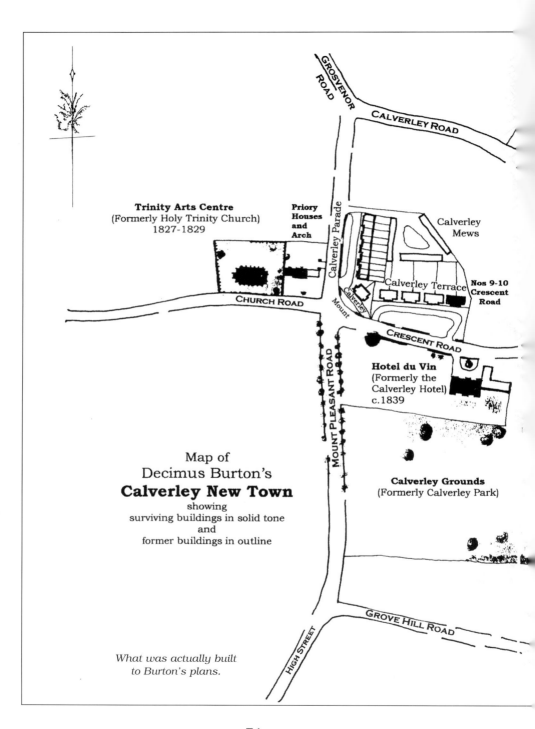

Map of
Decimus Burton's
Calverley New Town
showing
surviving buildings in solid tone
and
former buildings in outline

*What was actually built
to Burton's plans.*

Trinity Arts Centre
(Formerly Holy Trinity Church)
1827-1829

Priory
Houses
and
Arch

Calverley
Mews

Calverley Terrace

Nos 9-10
Crescent
Road

CHURCH ROAD

CRESCENT ROAD

Hotel du Vin
(Formerly the
Calverley Hotel)
c.1839

Calverley Grounds
(Formerly Calverley Park)

GROSVENOR ROAD

CALVERLEY ROAD

Calverley Parade

Calverley Mount

MOUNT PLEASANT ROAD

HIGH STREET

GROVE HILL ROAD

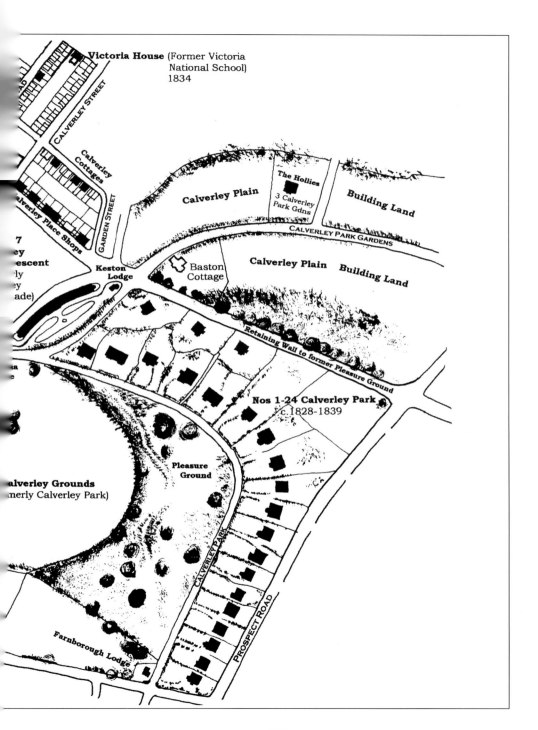

Victoria House (Former Victoria National School) 1834

CALVERLEY STREET

Calverley Cottages

alverley Place Shops

GARDEN STREET

7
ey
escent
ly
ey
ade)

Keston Lodge

Baston Cottage

Calverley Plain

The Hollies

3 Calverley Park Gdns

Building Land

CALVERLEY PARK GARDENS

Calverley Plain

Building Land

Retaining Wall to former Pleasure Ground

Nos 1-24 Calverley Park
c.1828-1839

Pleasure Ground

CALVERLEY PARK

alverley Grounds
merly Calverley Park)

PROSPECT ROAD

Farnborough Lodge

The twenty-four villas in Calverley Park are arranged in a landscaped setting around a Pleasure Ground, bringing the Regent's Park concept of a Residential Park on a smaller scale to Tunbridge Wells. Each villa is an architectural gem in its own right. Although the villas vary in style, some being Italianate, some Old English and some Regency "Gothick", they are similar in scale and materials, and form a wonderfully homogeneous and intact ensemble.

View of Calverley Park.

No. 1 Calverley Park. An Italianate Villa with an over-hanging eave and triple round-arched window.

Nos. 3 and 4 Calverley Park. Villas in the Old English style, with decorative barge boards.

No. 7 Calverley Park. An archetypal Regency Villa.

Close by is Calverley Park Crescent of circa 1833. This was formerly known as Calverley Promenade and, although now residential, it was originally designed as a shopping precinct, with a covered colonnade, to provide facilities for the New Town similar to those on The Pantiles.

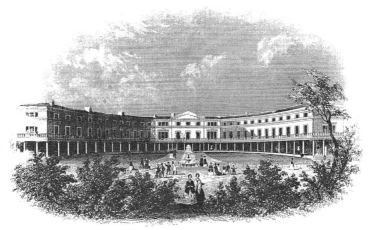

Calverley Park Crescent in 1860.

Further shops were provided in Calverley Place, now Nos. 57-79 Calverley Road, in the form of a series of linked pavilions. The pavilions still survive in a recognisable form, although the single-storied linking shops have been changed in various ways over the years.

Calverley Place, Nos. 57-59 Calverley Road.
Messrs. Bramah's Counting House was in the Central Pavilion.

Behind Calverley Place, three pairs of cottages also survive. Calverley Road, of course, is now the town's main shopping street, and the two shopping centres of the New and Old Towns have been linked into a single entity.

Calverley Park Gardens formed part of Decimus Burton's original layout for the New Town, his own "Cottage Ornée", Baston Cottage, has long since gone, and only The Hollies at No.3 may have been designed by him. Most of Calverley Park Gardens came to be developed in the 1850s by the able figure of William Willicombe (1800-1875). Born in Bath, Willicombe came to Tunbridge Wells in 1829 and began his career with Messrs.Bramah[8], being involved with them in the erection of the Calverley Park Villas, The Crescent, Calverley Terrace, Calverley Parade and Calverley Place. Much of the later development of the Calverley Estate fell to William Willicombe to undertake on his own account, including Lansdowne Road, most of Sandrock Road and part of Pembury Road.

The establishment of Calverley Park in the late 1820s and 1830s, together with the coming of the railway in the 1840s, acted as something of an encouragement for other landowners to follow suit. As can be seen from the map below, the town became ringed by a series of Residential Parks. Some of these, such as Camden Park, featured an area of open parkland, while others, such as Boyne Park, were spacious sylvan residential streets. It is, however, to Messrs. Ward, Burton and Bramah, followed by Willicombe, that Tunbridge Wells owes much of its character, and its metamorphosis from a summer resort to a residential town.

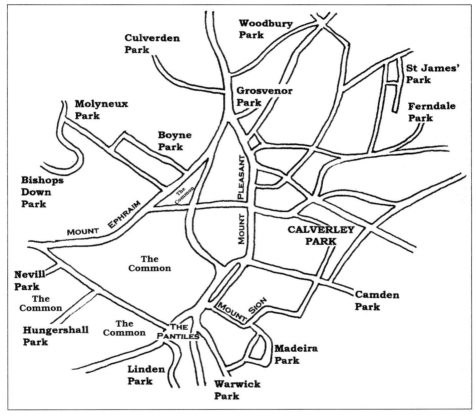

The Residential Parks of Tunbridge Wells.

79

THE GROWTH OF POPULATION AND THE LOCAL ECONOMY, AND THE RULE OF THE COMMISSIONERS, 1835-1889

by Lionel Anderson

By the beginning of the 19th century, Tunbridge Wells had changed from a village with a very seasonal population into one with a growing permanent population, which over the first 30 years of the century began to match and then outstrip that of its near neighbour and overlord, Tonbridge. The population of Tunbridge Wells increased nearly five-fold between 1800 and by 1831 there was an urgent need for a programme of works to develop the infrastructure necessary to deal with this significant increase in population. But, it was not until an Act of Parliament in 1835, when special powers were granted to Commissioners, that it proved possible for the town to control its own destiny rather than just form a part of Tonbridge Parish.

The early Victorian years witnessed economic boom and bust, the arrival of the railway age, a headlong rush into industrialization, exploding birth rates, rapid urbanisation, and growing radicalism leading to reform of the political system. As the century progressed the role of religious groups particularly the Non-conformists played an important role in the development of political parties and we see the emergence of the middle and working classes. In short it was "a period of great change in British society both politically and socially".[1]

Even before the passing of the Reform Act (of 1832) a spirit of revolution was in the air. The French Revolution and the Napoleonic wars had meant major change for most major European nations, but this was not the case in England with its monarchy and institutions still in place. But there were growing numbers of radicals many, no doubt, influenced by events in France now agitating for social and political change. And, at times of poor economic conditions they found ready support from the labouring class. With the authorities becoming increasingly alarmed at the rise of political activity by the working-class movement many public meetings were banned. But on August 16 1819 a mass meeting of workers demanding parliamentary reform ended in tragedy when a number of the demonstrators were killed as a result of action taken by the yeomanary. Known as the massacre of 'Peterloo' this event had a profound impact on all levels of society.

The protest movement was not confined simply to factory workers and city dwellers. Between 1829-1832 throughout most of Kent and Sussex gangs of farm workers and labourers were roaming the countryside burning barns and hayricks and destroying the newly introduced threshing machines. These disturbances known as the "Swing Riots" were not so much a political movement, but rather a direct consequence of high unemployment (partly caused by high immigration of Irish labour), rising food prices, the "tithe system", and the growing poverty of the labouring class. This point was echoed by the *Kentish Gazette* which reported 'The origins of these outrages is from no political feeling but from 'great and dire distress'[2]. Such was the concern of the authorities that a Line Cavalry Regiment (the 5th Dragoon Guards) were based in Tunbridge Wells to police West Kent and Sussex.

The first real step towards political reform was the passage of the first Reform Act of 1832, which eliminated many anomalies such as 'rotten boroughs' and enfranchised the new industrial towns, hitherto unrepresented. More importantly, it was recognition by Parliament of the growing strength of the mercantile classes who were demanding a greater involvement in the running of the state. As Lord Grey said "the principles of my reform are to prevent the necessity for revolution".

At the beginning of this period, Tunbridge Wells was a relatively small town with no real history of radicalism when compared, say, to the main centres of population and industry in the County such as Maidstone, Gravesend and Rochester. However, it did share one common feature with them and that was a population explosion.

A brief look at the years from 1800 to 1831 is useful in gaining some perspective, although obtaining figures for this earlier period present difficulties as Tunbridge Wells was then part of the parish of Tonbridge and included parts of Rusthall and Frant. Chalklin estimates a population of around 1200 in 1801 and the table shows the growth and size of the population of Tunbridge Wells, Tonbridge and Maidstone from this date to 1831.[3]

TABLE 1 COMPARATIVE POPULATIONS

	Tunbridge Wells	Tonbridge	Maidstone	Kent
1801	1,200e			
1821	2,000	5,406e	12,508	426,016
1831	5,929	4,451	15,790	478,028

e = estimate   Note: The figure for Tunbridge Wells in 1821 is based on the register of baptisms recorded at King Charles Chapel.

Source: National Census and Estimates.

From this table, it can be seen that the town's population was increasing at a very fast rate (albeit from a low base) when compared to Tonbridge, Maidstone and the County as a whole. In fact the population of Tonbridge actually declined over this period. In the years from 1831 there are again marked differences when compared to Tonbridge. As the table below illustrates, between 1831 and 1841 there was a 40% increase in the population of Tunbridge Wells, whereas in Tonbridge a further decline occurred.

TABLE 2 LATER COMPARATIVE POPULATIONS

	Tunbridge Wells	Tonbridge	Maidstone	Kent
1841	8,302	4,228	18,086	548,177
1851	10,587	5,961	20,801	615,766
1861	13,807	7,197	23,058	733,887
1871	19,410	8,189	26,237	848,294
1881	24,309	9,342	29,623	
1891	27,895	10,123	32,145	

Source: Census Returns.

Economic conditions were very poor at this time and in Tonbridge there were serious health problems with the outbreak of cholera and smallpox, which may well be the reason for this somewhat surprising decline at a time when population numbers were generally rising rapidly. However, in the following ten year period the population of Tonbridge recovered but it never matched that of Tunbridge Wells. This particular ten-year period covers the arrival of the railway in 1845 and it would appear that Tonbridge, which was a main terminus for the Wealden line, owes its revival as much to that factor as any other.

The figures shown in the Tables above raise an interesting question – why did Tunbridge Wells grow so quickly in the first 50 years of the 19th century and also sustain a relatively high rate of population growth? The reasons for the high population growth in Tunbridge Wells are not difficult to find.

From the end of the 18th. century, the town began to attract a new breed of resident – the annuitant – men and women of independent means. Many retiring officers from the Army and Navy and former Government officials, particularly from the East India Company, who had spent years abroad were now seeking a residence which suited their life styles: Tunbridge Wells together with towns like Bath and Cheltenham was the "in place". This influx of moneyed people in turn led to a large demand for domestic labour. The census return for 1841 for Calverley Park, Calverley Gardens and Terrace reveals that the ratio of owners (plus family) to servants was 1: 1.44. By 1881 this ratio had risen close to 2. Heads of Households of properties in the areas mentioned were classified mainly as annuitants, clergy or magistrates and nearly half were female, many widowed.

Besides information on the size of population the census returns of 1841, 1861 and 1881 also provide useful information as to how the town's working population was employed. According to Chalklin, in his study of the 1841 census, some 3,000 of the town's population of 8,302 were registered as working. Over half this number were manual workers and with over 1,000 servants living in Tunbridge Wells at that time, servants represented about a third of the estimated working population[4]. The remainder were generally involved or connected to the requirements of the leisured and professional classes.

The 1861 census begins to reflect the impact of the "railway age" with new occupations such as Railwaymen, Railway Policemen, Booking Clerks, Ticket Collectors, Switchmen and Railway Drivers making an appearance. Growing levels of prosperity and improved living standards also become apparent with new occupations registered such as Gas Fitters, Stonemasons, Landscape Gardeners, Importer of Foreign Wines, Telegraph Messengers, Printers, and last but not least the local Inspector of Taxes. Besides the domestic staff required to maintain the life style of this rich enclave we can also see the emergence of the professional classes in the form of doctors, bankers, solicitors, architects and the estate agents or, as they were known then, "house agents".

A study of local Trade Directories is a useful source of reference in gaining some insight as to how the local economy developed over this period. The table below starts in 1845 the year of the arrival of the railway when the economy was beginning to recover from the depression years of 1837-1842. It illustrates the number of tradesmen/shopkeepers operating in those trades that might be considered as offering "the basic necessities of life". The same trades are examined again in 1862 and 1886 to highlight where significant changes have occurred in the numbers and which may signify changing patterns of demand and size of population:

TABLE 3 No. OF ESTABLISHMENTS LISTED IN VARIOUS TRADE DIRECTORIES

	1845	1861	1886
Butcher	21	24	46
Baker	11	20	33
Coal Merchants	6	8	46
Dairyman	5	7	28
Grocer	15	20	72
Fly Proprietor	3	9	25
Tobacconist	1	6	18
Beer Retailer	7	23	62

Source: Post Office Directory – 1845; Kelly's Directory -1861; Tunbridge Wells Directory – 1886.

One of the interesting changes to note is the relative movement of Butchers and Bakers in the sixteen years to 1861. Why should this be? We can be reasonably certain that unlike today's society a fall in meat demand was not due to a change in dietary habits. More likely these figures reflect a growing "poor" population in the town. To some extent this view is borne out by the large number of labourers in the 1861 census. A growing poor population is also evident from the writings of Benge Burr who, earlier in the century had called on the great Abergavenny estate to release some of their forest land on the south of the town for smallholdings for the subsistence of 'innumerable families of the industrious poor'.[5]

Larkin, the family butcher in Chapel Place.

The fortunes of the Butchers seems to have revived in the years from 1861-1886 with an increase in numbers from 24 to 46, suggesting growing prosperity in the town as the middle class expanded. The growth in Beer Retailers in both periods (there were also some 28 Wine and Spirit merchants in 1886) is also of interest. Hard drinking, like obesity was thought to be an indicator of physical strength in those days and was a major problem for the authorities. In 1870 a group of West Kent Clergy stated 'there is hardly a town or village where the number of public houses is not in excess of reasonable requirement'[6]. The problem of drunkenness faced every Watch Committee in the land. Often their own police forces who, when patrolling their beat visited these establishments, were as inebriated as the best of them. Indeed, even respectable Tunbridge Wells had its problems – in July 1837 three out of the five constables in the town were suspended for drunkenness.[7]

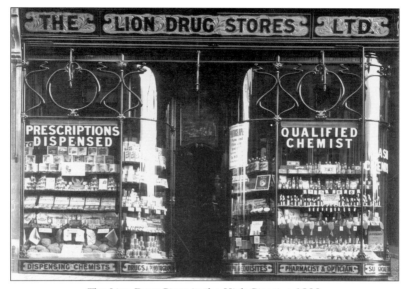

The Lion Drug Store in the High Street, c.1900.

From 1861 there were large increases in a numbers of trades/services reflecting the basic needs of a growing population and the requirements of a wealthy, but ageing, segment of the towns population. For example, there were now 53 boot/shoe makers (including Freeman Hardy Willis on Mt. Pleasant), 35 Paper Hangers, 9 Bath Chair dealers, 6 Tea Dealers, 42 Confectioners and Pastry Cooks, and 15 Coffee/Dining establishments. The same survey indicates a revival in coach builders to eight, a trade which virtually vanished after the railway arrived, and a further decline in the fortunes of Tunbridge Ware Manufacturers. For some reason Straw Bonnet Makers, of which there were six in 1841, had virtually disappeared by 1861 – perhaps the ladies were shopping in London by then.

The other main trade that warrants comment is the Hotel/Lodging Business, which experienced a further revival by 1886. Although contemporary records indicate good growth from 1845 that year actually marked the nadir of its fortunes from earlier years. In the earlier part of the century the town's lodging house industry had been considerably stronger as witnessed by Barrow's 1808 map showing 137 lodging houses. The fall in the trade during the earlier period reflects the fashion for sea bathing and the recovery after 1845 is due to the arrival of the railway.

High Street, Tunbridge Wells, c.1870.

The information contained in the Trade Directories certainly helps in the understanding of everyday life in this growing town, the manner in which business developed and how the needs of the community were met.

The Commissioners

With fast rising populations the quality of life in the town was deteriorating rapidly by the early 19th century. In the winter months people were ankle deep in mud and horse manure, the sewer system was unable to cope, there was an inadequate supply of fresh water, which together with poor housing meant real dangers to public health. And on top of these problems, law and order (mainly drink related) was causing considerable disquiet amongst the populace.

Before 1835 Tunbridge Wells had no formal local government, being divided between the parishes of Tonbridge, Speldhurst and Frant. In the early days of its fame as a seasonal spa resort, informal arrangements by residents and visitors had been sufficient to fill this gap, but as the residential population grew people began to feel the need for a properly constituted local authority. Concerns about law and order led in 1816 to the establishment of an Association for Prosecuting Felons, and in 1832 a committee of residents called for better drainage and sewerage.

On 28 October 1833, a 'general meeting of ratepayers and proprietors' met at the Sussex Hotel and voted to set up a twenty-one member committee to explore the possibility of 'obtaining an Act of Parliament for lighting and watching (i.e. policing) Tunbridge Wells'. The committee's efforts led in 1835 to the appointment of a body of Commissioners under an Act of Parliament for 'lighting, watching (i.e. policing), cleansing, regulating and otherwise improving the town of Tunbridge Wells in the county of Kent and Sussex and for regulating the supply of water and establishing a market within the said town'.

Front page of the Minute Book of Tunbridge Wells Local Act Committee.

The minute book of the Local Act Committee provides a fascinating insight into the workings of this body as they attempt to establish the town's first local government. The minute books also throw a little light on some of the political hurdles they faced and the somewhat unusual manner in which Decimus Burton was involved in the negotiations between the parties. It is clear from the proposals set out that, although there would be significant benefits for the residents of the town, the plan would need the approval of the main landowners. As the minutes show, there were battles to be fought before the infrastructure of Tunbridge Wells could be improved.

Between 1833 and 1835, the Local Act Committee met regularly to discuss the detailed process of obtaining the proposed Act of Parliament. On 11 November 1833, they agreed to restrict membership of the Commissioners to thirty-one, and to those having a minimum annual income from rents of £50. At a meeting on 7 November, they studied estimates of the relative expenses of lighting the town with oil or gas lamps and decided that the latter, at £495, would be the most efficient. At the same time they looked at the costs of four night watchmen (£165) and four daytime police (£156). At the meeting on 11 December, they felt it would be a mark of respect to advise John Ward, Major Gardner, the Marquess Camden and the Earl of Abergavenny of their decisions and actions. Furthermore, it was decided to make copies of their report available to the public and for it to be advertised in *The Visitor*. In December, according to *The Visitor*, there was a fracas in the town with the burning of an effigy: Chalklin speculates it might have been John Ward.[8]

This speculation by Chalklin is probably correct for in the minutes of a meeting in early February the Committee hear from Ward that he is not prepared to approve the plan as he considers that important information has been withheld by the solicitors acting for the committee. A tactful letter was dispatched suggesting he might attend a meeting 'to remove many of the mistakes and misconstructions, which have arisen'.

Not surprisingly, as the owner of 874 acres of the Calverley Estate, Ward clearly had his own agenda for already a development plan of some 56 acres had already been laid out by Decimus Burton.[9] This becomes apparent from the minutes of a meeting of 17th February at which the Chairman reads a letter from Ward in which he states that if his Estate is excluded from the operation of the Bill "he would subscribe to the Act for the rest of the plan". Otherwise he would fight the Bill. (Mr Ward at this time not only owned Calverley Estate, but had been MP for Leominster and was High Sheriff for Kent.)[10] In response the Committee felt that they had no authority to allow for such an exclusion of this property; that too much time had been lost and they felt compelled to press on with the first reading of the Bill; and that a public meeting of the ratepayers should be called to discuss the position.

The minutes of a meeting held on the 6th March indicate that the Earl of Abergavenny is backing John Ward. But, to the credit of the Committee, they move a resolution which stated "this committee are of the opinion that the Earl of Abergavenny has sanctioned Mr. Ward's claim from an imperfect knowledge of the true localities of his Estate as connected with those particular parts of the town where lighting and watching are of utmost importance".[11] This somewhat challenging statement to the premier landowner of the district indicates that an element of democracy is at work amongst the committee, which now consists not simply of the gentry, but also business people intent on improving the town's infrastructure. This approach seems to have worked, for at the next meeting on the 27th March, a sub-committee meets with Mr. Ward's solicitors who put forward a proposal that if the Committee postponed the Bill until the next session of Parliament, certain pledges would be made by Ward. Some of these pledges are listed below, and one in particular is of importance, for it determines the geographic manner in which Tunbridge Wells would grow in the future:

- ❖ £100 will be spent on drainage around his Estate.

- ❖ Mr. Ward will pay one-half of the expenses of the Bill

- ❖ Clauses to be inserted to prevent hawking within 20 roads of the markets

- ❖ Boundaries to be defined precisely

- ❖ Not to borrow more than £2000

And of most interest is the recognition that the privacy of certain properties in the town, such as Nevill and Calverley Parks, were to be respected, and Grove Hill was to be screened if possible. These proposals were agreed to by the Committee and on the 10th May the minutes confirmed the receipt of £100 from Ward for drainage work. At the same meeting, a sub-committee consisting of James Fry, James Richardson and Decimus Burton were appointed to superintend the drainage.

The sudden appearance of Decimus Burton's name is somewhat surprising for it does not appear that he was ever appointed as a member of the main committee at any time. At a meeting on 25th August another sub- committee was formed to draw up agreed boundary lines and Decimus Burton was included in this group. So we have a situation where Decimus Burton was appointed to two sub-committees (in his absence) and has never been appointed as a member of the main Committee. Given Burton's involvement with Ward, it seems reasonable to assume that Ward was insisting on his involvement but even if this is the case, it does not explain why he was not officially appointed to the committee.

On the 14th October, Burton attends a committee meeting which was concerned with boundary issues. Decimus Burton was also present on 6th March 1835 when the subject was again about boundaries and at which a further three members were appointed to the original group set-up to examine boundaries. It is surprising that Decimus Burton was present when the all-important subject of boundaries was being considered, since they might well have compromised his plans. It is of interest that when this committee reported back on the 20th March 1835, Decimus Burton was not mentioned as a signatory to the report. It would appear that political expediency was at work and overruled the normal manner in which the committee conducted its business.

At the last meeting of this committee on the 27th June 1835, we learn that the Earl of Abergavenny had refused to pay the additional fees required. Despite this, the solicitors were directed to proceed with the Bill according to the resolution passed on 14th May.

The next part of this saga was the formation of the Tunbridge Wells Commissioners on 27th July 1835. Seventy-nine males were present to take the oath of qualification as required under the Act: the requirement being property ownership and a rental income of not less than £50 p.a. Membership was across the social spectrum with members of the gentry, professionals and tradesmen. Amongst the names appearing were those of Decimus Burton of Baston Cottage, Calverley Estate (who never attended a meeting); Charles Cripps; and William Delves who it seems was a member of this body for some years; together with James Elliot (Butcher), Cuthbert Webb (Grocer), and Stephen Beeching (Banker).

The Committee met for the first time at the Clarence Tavern, but decided that future meetings should be held at Vale Cottage and they authorised suitable furniture for the proposed Police Station at No.2, Mount Pleasant.

This Committee worked quickly and diligently and by August 1835 had resolved the importance of procuring the town to be lighted with Gas and for a Police Committee to be appointed. At the September meeting, they agreed to pay for two lamplighters a weekly wage of 15 shillings and Tenders were placed for the lighting of the town. By October, they had moved on to cleaning and requested anyone willing to contact a scavenger for the collection of all rubbish, filth soil but not dung. At the same meeting tenders were agreed with Josh Webb for the lighting; and the services of a scavenger (Thomas Marchant) were approved for a sum of £75 p.a.

The Tunbridge Wells Police Force, 1874. (21 in total)

Watching (i.e. policing) was a major responsibility for the Committee, but strangely there are no references to the number of policemen appointed, of their hours of duty, or the area they covered; but plenty of discussion about the cost of uniforms bought in London, which led to uniforms being handed down, although the line was drawn about handing down boots as well.

What were the policing problems facing this rapidly expanding town?

❖ Obstruction of pavements by shopkeepers' displays and low-hanging signs (Richard Mace had his path blocked by the barrels of oyster-sellers).
❖ House and drive gates then often opened outwards, causing understandable problems.
❖ Innumerable parking offences – of carriages, delivery carts, gout- and bath-chairs, and dog-carts.
❖ Dangerous driving (of horses, carriages, wagons and carts) and even road-rage, although it was not called that.
❖ Drunkenness which was not confined to the public – the main reason for police dismissal was being drunk or asleep on duty.
❖ Manure of every sort carted at the 'wrong' time of day.
❖ Prostitution and noisy gatherings were a feature of the Pantiles.
❖ Even hoop-trundling, and later football, became a minor offence if played in the street.

It would seem that Bonfire Night – November 5th – was a particular problem for the police and the fire brigade. The Committee directed the whole of the police force to be on duty on the 5th November 1836. On 6th November, 6 people were taken into custody for 'firing' fireworks on the Parade (The Pantiles). They were each fined two shillings and sixpence (12½p.) During the arrest procedure of three of the men, stones were thrown at the police and firemen, by a crowd estimated at between 200-300 (a large number for a town with a population of about 7,000).

By 1851, the annual records of the Committee were more formal:

❖ No. of prisoners taken: 367
❖ Police pay increases –
Constables from 18/- (90p.) to 19/- (95p) a week (£45 at 2005 values).
Sergeants from 22/-(£1.10) to 24/-(£1.20) a week. (£56 at 2005 values).
Superintendent from 35/- (£1.75) to £2 a week. (£95 at 2005 values).

- ❖ The Police Station had moved to the Calverley Market site.
- ❖ Punishments were harsh: 7 years' imprisonment for stealing £19 (£855 at 2005 values).
- ❖ Transportation for life (to Australia) for burglary and stealing lead.

Other aspects of the necessary infrastructure of a growing town were recorded:

- ❖ The Gas Company was formed in 1843.

The Gas Works, Upper Grosvenor Road.

- ❖ The Town Fire Service was inaugurated in 1845, with the fire-engine and equipment being stored at No.11 Calverley Mews.

The Volunteer Fire Brigade, 1880.

❖ September 1864 saw the start of long, complicated and frequently acrimonious negotiations to form a Municipal Water Supply Company, drawing on a number of privately-owned springs belonging to the principal landowners, the Earl of Abergavenny, Marquess Camden and the Ward family.

The Engine Room of the Waterworks at Pembury.

❖ The General Hospital was rebuilt in 1869
❖ Although Tunbridge Wells had had a number of newspapers before, it is worth recording that the *Kent & Sussex Courier* was first published in 1872.
❖ The Eye and Ear Hospital was established in 1878
❖ A telephone exchange was opened in 1887.

Horse drawn bus in Tunbridge Wells, c.1900.

The minutes of the many meetings held by the Commissioners provides an intriguing insight into the multifarious issues which affected local society in those days and how little some of these issues have changed over the years. For example, the reports by the Police Committee: in early 1836, the police are seen to be dealing with individuals on matters not connected with the peace of the town and they (the police) were instructed to enforce the printed regulations. In the same year the Committee resolved "that as the police force is so very small compared with the great extent of the town, the Magistrate be respectfully requested to abstain as much as possible from directing warrants to be served by the Policemen when the Parish Constables, *a quite different, but lower, level of enforcement* are able to perform this duty, as it will otherwise be impossible for the Police Commission to carry into effect the regulations adopted by the Commissioners".

Another example is the report by a Sub-Committee of Assessors who stated in their report of 5th December 1836 that "your committee have with great labour and pain gone through the entire assessment of 1835 and endeavoured to the best of their judgement to equalise any apparent disproportion in the relative value of houses – and it will afford great satisfaction to your committee if the result of their labours should meet with a favourable reception from the public."

The Commissioners' role was a very varied one and the work was broken down under various sub-committees. These dealt with trade disputes – particularly over the hire of carriages; assaults against the police, for which there was a 2-month imprisonment and hard labour; setting the rates; dealing with licences; settling disputes over drains and sewers; and law and order. Although the Board of Commissioners was in theory a more democratic system, as Savidge comments, it was a self-perpetuating oligarchy. By comparison, Tonbridge remained under the even-more oligarchic control of its Parish Vestry until 1870, when a body of Improvement Commissioners were appointed.

But the Tunbridge Wells structure was unsuited to an expanding town. Minor changes had been achieved by the Town Improvement Act of 1846, which tightened procedures, redefined some boundaries and abolished turnpike trusts, but management was still in the hands of a select and somewhat reactionary few. By 1860, when the population had grown to almost 14,000, the number of people eligible to be Commissioners had grown to 200-300.[12] Despite this, it was difficult to get a quorum of seven for meetings of the Commissioners. Reformers, including the Rector of Frant who was Abergavenny's brother-in-law and William Delves who was his Steward, forced through at public meetings in 1860 the elective clauses of the Local Government Act of 1858.

As a result, the number of Commissioners was fixed at 24, one third to be elected annually and the voting qualification was reduced to owning or occupying land worth £30 a year. But it was not a straight vote of one man, one vote. The greater the value of your land, the more votes you had, rising to a maximum of six, so there was a strong bias to the larger landowner.

This 'improvement' was to last nearly thirty years, but from 1881 when the population had increased to over 24,000, there was growing pressure for reform, particularly from the Tradesmen's Association. Eight stormy years later, with the Incorporation of Tunbridge Wells as a Borough, democracy came to at least the male, and also a few female, ratepayers of the new Borough.

The Town Hall telephone in 1901.

Whether Incorporation stimulated the inhabitants into becoming far-sighted, progressive and innovative; or whether they were already so, which is why they achieved Incorporation, is difficult to say. But certainly the 10-15 years which followed Incorporation were probably the most stimulating in the town's history. The Council somewhat unconventionally appointed far-sighted and pro-active Mayors, such as Sir David Salomons, Bt. (in 1894-5), and Major J.R. Fletcher Lutwidge (three times in 1895-6, 1896-7 and 1901-2), who were not actually members of the Council; opened their own Borough Electricity Works in 1895; introduced electric street lighting subsequently; set up the first municipal telephone system in England in 1901 (long before Kingston-upon-Hull); and approved the building of a new theatre for Tunbridge Wells, called for tactful reasons the Opera House, which opened in 1902. These were stimulating times for everyone in Tunbridge Wells.[13]

Cartouche of Thomas Stidolph's Map of Tunbridge Wells in 1838.
Note that it refers to the Local Act District, and to Stidolph
as Surveyor to the Commissioners.

CHAPTER 9

THE RAILWAY AND TUNBRIDGE WELLS
(1846-2005)

by John Arkell

Before the arrival of the railway, the best means of access to Tunbridge Wells was the Turnpike road for which tolls were charged. It was supposed to be (and generally was) well-kept and was used by the mail coaches, for whom speed was the essence. By comparison, local roads were maintained by the parish and were usually muddy in winter and dusty in summer; and full of pot-holes and ruts.

The only other means was by river. Parts of the River Medway were converted to a canal at the end of the 17th. century, built to provide a means of heavy transport to and from the Weald area; and it was used to ship in coal and manufactured goods and ship out timber. The first Act of Parliament for the Medway Navigation, as the canal was called, was passed in 1664 and the Navigation was opened in about 1750. There were further Acts making improvements to the Navigation in 1802 and 1824. But it was never a means, or meant to be a means, of passenger transportation. It was originally intended to extend the canal to Penshurst and construction of some of it was started about 1829 and then abandoned. The earthworks can still be seen in the vicinity of the Leigh Barrier.

Elsewhere in the country, tramroads using mainly horses as motive power had been constructed to connect with canal systems. These were seen as an improvement on the roads, since by running on rails, traffic did not get bogged down in winter when the roads turned to mud. An early scheme was to connect Tunbridge Wells to the Canal by tramroad. A tunnel was proposed under Mount Ephraim, but never carried out. However, tramroads were designed essentially for freight, and not passengers.

The years after the defeat of Napoleon in 1815 were difficult years for employment – the Industrial Revolution had been underway since about 1760 but in any period of change, supply and demand are rarely in equilibrium and supply of labour often exceeded demand. As a result, there was a large degree of social unrest (stimulated amongst other things, by the ideas of the French Revolution, less than 30 years previously, and the number of soldiers now demobbed) which lead to outbursts such as the Peterloo massacre in Manchester on 16 August

1819, in which 11 were killed and over 500 injured, and in Kent, the Swing riots in the late 1820's and early 1830's.

The first passenger and freight railway was the Stockton & Darlington Railway in 1825. It was followed in 1830 by the Canterbury & Whitstable line, just ahead of the Liverpool and Manchester Railway, which was followed by an explosive period of development. By 1847, over 250,000 navvies were employed in railway construction.

The railways tapped into this mobile pool of labour which moved from contract to contract, living in temporary hutted encampments. Labour and life was cheap and much of the work was done by nothing more than horse, man and barrow. Even more labour became available after the Irish potato famine (1845-51).

In 1838, the main way of travel from London to Tunbridge Wells was by stage-coach, a journey of 36 miles via Sevenoaks, which took six-eight hours each way. Nevertheless, an estimated 11,000 made the (return) journey in a season (April- November), an average of 175 people travelled each week in each direction. These figures imply that there were about 2 coaches, seating twelve, each way per day over the eight-month season.

Several schemes for railway development south of London were put before Parliament, but the one that eventually gained an Act of Parliament in the last year of the reign of William IV on 21st June 1836, was that destined to become the South Eastern Railway (SER). Parliament decided in its wisdom that there would only ever be a need for one route south out of the capital; and so instructed the London and Brighton Railway and the London and Dover Railway to share tracks over the existing London & Croydon Railway as far as Croydon and thence south to Reigate Junction (later Redhill), from where the South Eastern's line would turn east to Dover via Tonbridge. This original route was $49\frac{1}{2}$ miles from London to Tunbridge Wells,once the branch was opened, but was quicker and cheaper than the shorter stagecoach route.

Building of the line commenced in 1837. The construction workers were known as 'navvies', which was short for navigators, as many of them had been employed previously on the construction of the canals. Relationships with the local landowners were never easy, especially when the navvies were caught poaching and some men were sacked in 1839 by the Inspector in charge of the Tonbridge section. The Medway Navigation was used to deliver rails and other materials to Tonbridge in 1841, in effect sealing its own fate. Decimus Burton was engaged to provide architectural advice to the contractor Cubitt. The navvies celebrated Christmas 1841 with a riot at Godstone during which a constable was injured. There were other occasions of bare-knuckle fighting between miners and bricklayers working on the tunnels in the Tunbridge Wells area during 1846. The small town police force had trouble maintaining order, breaking up the fights and dispersing the crowds of onlookers and the men known as the 'Fancy', or betting community.

The SER was hoping to start running trains to Tonbridge by May 1842. They placed several orders for carriages. Opening day was 26th May 1842 and the service started with four trains each way per day. It was initially decided not to run trains on Sundays, but this decision was reversed by July 1842, the explanation being 'public necessity'.

Initial traffic was disappointing, but this was mainly due to the line not yet being complete as far as Dover. The stations which opened with the line were Redhill, Godstone, Edenbridge, Penshurst, and Tonbridge. The line as far as Headcorn was opened on 31st August 1842 and to Ashford by 1st December. A special train was run in connection with the opening to Ashford. It took three and a half hours to travel from London Bridge, due to stops for the inspecting officer.

Folkestone was reached on 28th June 1843. A service of seven trains each way per day was introduced, the fastest taking 3hrs 5 minutes to reach Folkestone. Finally Dover was reached on 7th February 1844.

Before the railway arrived in the area, the post in West Kent was carried by the London-to-Hastings Mailcoach for distribution by post offices along the route. After Dover was reached by rail in 1844, a start was made on the 10th May to transfer some of the post to the South Eastern Railway. Hastings and part of the Dover mail, including the foreign mails and Deal Ship Letters, were to be sent by train. In consequence, many changes were made to deliveries in the Hastings division. Staplehurst and Hurst Green were made Post Towns; and the London-to-Hastings Mailcoach now ran only between Hastings and the Post Office at the railway station at Staplehurst; and a mailcart ran from Staplehurst to Rye. At the same time, Foots Cray and Lamberhurst which were staging posts on the routes to Hastings and Dover respectively, were discontinued. However, the Dover Night Mail and the Dover Day Mail continued to run by road, serving the towns to the north of Kent.

From Monday 27th January 1845, Day mailbags were made up for the following towns: – Tunbridge (sic), Tunbridge Wells, Sevenoaks, Ashford, Folkestone and Dover, all enclosed in a sack labelled "Reigate and

Dover". Mail for Staplehurst, Cranbrook, Hurst Green, Battle, St Leonards, and Hastings was enclosed in a sack labelled "Staplehurst and Hastings".

In April 1848, the first trial took place at Croydon of 'Dicker's improved apparatus'. This equipment allowed mailbags to be picked up and set down whilst the train was moving. These trials were so successful that additional apparatus was installed at New Cross and Edenbridge. From 1st Sept 1848, Edenbridge was made a Post Town and the minute in the Post Office record states "bags must be made up for both night and day mails and given to the guard of the Dover mail". Attached was a list of "Places, Gentlemen's Seats, and Principle (sic) Houses in the Delivery of Edenbridge".

During 1843, plans were being made by the SER to add a line to Tunbridge Wells. No time was lost, their chief engineer Barlow produced a plan and on 28th May the SER decided to go ahead with it. By 25th June, a contract for construction had been let and by August, the SER was buying up land between Tonbridge and Robertsbridge – all this before any authorisation from Parliament. This haste was due to wanting to stop penetration eastwards by the Brighton company who were intent on reaching Hastings. The Tunbridge Wells branch was authorised by Parliament in the 1844-45 session.

The Colebrook Viaduct c.1847.

The first Tunbridge Wells station was a temporary one, constructed at Jackswood Springs, and opened on 20th September 1845. This was due to the Wells tunnel not being finished in time. The contractor had been delayed in the construction of the Wells tunnel by not being allowed to dig shafts and excavate the tunnel up the shafts. Work was only permitted from each end, as the spoil would otherwise have to have been carted through the streets of the town. What is now Tunbridge Wells Central Station was finally opened on 25th November 1846 and Jackswood Springs became the Goods Station.

Tunbridge Wells Central Railway Station c.1850.
Note the sidings where now there is car-parking.

A South Eastern Railway Timetable published on the 1st of December 1846 for the opening of the Margate branch has some interesting information on the service to Tunbridge Wells which had opened only the previous week. On weekdays (which included Saturdays) there were seven trains from London Bridge to Tunbridge Wells; and eight in the reverse direction. Of these, two trains up to London and one train in the down direction were 1st class expresses. Two more in each direction were 1st and 2nd class only; while 3rd class passengers were limited to a choice of only four trains each way per day. On Sundays, there were only four trains each way, all of which took all three classes. The fastest journey time for the first class express trains was 1hr 25mins, the fare for which was ten shillings and sixpence (£20 at 2005 values). The early morning all class 'parliamentary' train took two and a quarter hours and the third class fare was 3 shillings and tenpence (£7 at 2005 values).

DOWN TRAINS.

DAILY TRAINS. FROM LONDON BRIDGE. / **SUNDAY TRAINS. FROM LONDON BRIDGE.**

Dist. from London (Mls)	Station	1 — 1st 2nd 3d Class Parly. A.M.	2 — 1st 2d Class A.M.	3 — 1st 2d 3d Class A.M.	4 — MAIL 1st 3d Class A.M.	5 — 1st 2d 3d Class P.M.	6 — 1st 2d Class P.M.	7 — 1st Class EXPRESS P.M.	8 — 1st 2d 3d Class P.M.	9 — 1st 2nd 3rd Class P.M.	10 — MAIL 1st 2d Class P.M.	SUN 1 — 1st 2nd 3d Class Parly.	SUN 3 — 1st 2d 3d Class A.M.	SUN 6 — 1st 2d M Class P.M.	SUN 8 — 1st 2d 3d Class P.M.	SUN 10 — MAIL 1st 2d Cl. P.M.
0	Leave London Bridge ....at	7.30	8.30	9.30	11.30	1.30	1.30	4.30	5.30	6.30	8.30	7.30	9.30	3.30	5.30	8.30
11	Arrive at Croydon ....About	7.53	8.53	9.57	11.55	1.57	3.57	..	5.57	6.56	8.53	7.53	9.57	3.57	5.57	8.53
19	Merstham	8.16	..	10.18	..	2.18	4.18	..	6.18	7.18	..	8.16	10.18	4.18	6.18	..
21	Reigate	8.24	9.18	10.26	12.19	2.26	4.26	5. 4	6.26	7.25	9.18	8.24	10.26	4.26	6.26	9.18
27	Godstone	8.39	..	10.42	..	2.42	4.34	..	6.42	7.40	..	8.39	10.42	4.42	6.42	..
32	Edenbridge	8.51	9.41	10.55	12.42	2.55	4.45	..	6.55	7.53	..	8.51	10.55	4.55	6.55	..
37	Penshurst	9.4	..	11.10	..	3.10	4.58	..	7.10	8.7	..	9.4	11.10	5.10	7.10	..
41	Tunbridge	9.18	10.3	11.24	1.3	3.24	5.13	5.36	7.24	8.20	10.3	9.18	11.24	5.24	7.24	10.3
46	Tunbridge Wells	9.45	..	11.55	1.25	3.55	5.35	5.55	..	8.45	..	9.45	11.55	5.55	7.55	..
46	Paddock Wood	9.33	10.18	11.40	1.18	3.40	5.26	5.47	7.40	8.28	10.18	9.33	11.40	5.40	7.40	10.18
50	Yalding	9.46	..	11.54	..	3.54	..	..	..	8.37	..	9.46	11.54	5.54	7.54	..
51	Wateringbury	9.52	..	12.1	1.36	4.1	5.46	6.3	..	8.42	..	9.52	12.1	6.1	8.1	..
54	East Farleigh	10.3	..	12.12	..	4.12	..	..	..	8.49	..	10.3	12.12	6.12	8.12	..
56	Maidstone	10.15	..	12.25	1.55	4.25	6.5	6.15	..	9.0	..	10.15	12.25	6.25	8.25	..
51	Marden	9.46	..	11.53	..	3.53	..	..	7.53	..	..	9.46	11.53	5.53	7.53	..
53	Staplehurst	9.55	10.32	12.2	1.34	4.2	5.42	6.1	8.2	..	10.32	9.55	12.2	6.2	8.2	10.32
56	Headcorn	10.5	..	12.12	..	4.12	..	..	8.12	..	..	10.5	12.12	6.12	8.12	..
62	Pluckley	10.17	..	12.25	2.4	4.25	..	..	8.25	..	..	10.17	12.25	6.25	8.25	..
67	Ashford	10.30	11.2	12.39	2.4	4.39	6.13	6.23	8.39	..	11.2	10.30	12.39	6.39	8.39	11.2
72	Wye	10.48	11.20	12.53	2.20	4.53	..	..	8.53	..	..	10.48	12.53	6.53	8.53	..
76	Chilham	10.58	11.30	1.7	2.30	5.7	6.43	6.43	9.7	..	..	10.58	1.7	7.7	9.7	..
81	Canterbury	11.12	11.45	1.20	2.45	5.20	6.55	6.55	9.20	..	..	11.12	1.20	7.20	9.20	..
88	Grove Ferry	11.28	..	1.35	3.0	5.35	..	..	9.35	..	..	11.28	1.35	7.35	9.35	..
93	Minster	11.40	12.12	1.50	3.12	5.50	..	..	9.50	..	..	11.40	1.50	7.50	9.50	..
97	Ramsgate	12.0	12.30	2.10	3.30	6.10	7.30	7.30	10.10	..	..	12.0	2.10	8.10	10.10	..
101	Margate	12.10	12.40	2.20	3.40	6.20	7.40	7.40	10.40	..	..	12.20	2.20	8.20	10.26	..
75	Westenhanger and Hythe	10.50	11.23	1.3	2.24	5.3	6.38	..	9.3	..	..	10.50	1.3	7.3	9.3	..
82	Folkestone	11.10	11.44	1.25	2.45	5.25	6.59	6.48	9.25	..	11.42	11.10	1.25	7.25	9.25	11.42

Extract from 1846 timetable.

(The 'parliamentary' train, to be referred to later in Gilbert & Sullivan's Lord High Executioner song in 'The Mikado', was introduced by Gladstone's Railway Regulation Act of 1844 which compelled the railways to run cheap trains at fares of no more than a penny a mile. The Act also stipulated that all carriages should offer protection against the weather. [An early 3rd. class passenger on the Great Western had reputedly frozen to death in a roofless carriage]. The railway companies retaliated by running many of the 'parliamentary' trains at grossly inconvenient times, and by giving all other trains priority over them). A dog fare for over 25 miles was two shillings and sixpence (£5). The dog was not permitted to accompany the passengers, but had to travel in a special dog box in the guard's van.

FARES FROM LONDON.

Dist. from London	Station	PASSENGERS Express	1st Class	2d Class	3d Class	CARRIAGES Two wheels	Four wheels	HORSES One horse	2 horse (If One Property)	3 horses
		s. d.	s. d.	s. d.	s. d.	s. d.	s. d.	s. d.	s. d.	s. d.
0	London Bridge	..	..	..	..	..	..	..	..	
11	Croydon	..	2 0	1 6	0 11	..	..	..	..	
19	Merstham	..	3 6	2 6	1 7	8 0	12 0	8 0	12 0	16 0
21	Reigate	5 0	4 0	3 0	1 9	8 0	12 0	8 0	12 0	16 0
27	Godstone	..	5 0	4 0	2 3	10 6	15 6	10 6	15 6	20 6
32	Edenbridge	..	6 0	4 6	2 8	12 0	18 0	12 0	18 0	24 0
37	Penshurst	..	7 0	5 0	3 1	14 0	21 0	14 0	21 0	28 0
41	Tunbridge	9 6	7 6	5 6	3 5	15 6	23 6	15 6	23 6	31 0
40	Tunbridge Wells	10 6	8 6	6 6	3 10	17 6	26 0	17 6	26 0	34 6
46	Paddock Wood	10 6	8 6	6 6	3 10	17 6	26 0	17 6	26 0	34 6
50	Yalding									

Extract from 1846 Fares. Note the fares for carriages and horses.

The 400th anniversary of our town also coincides with the 160th anniversary of the opening of our station. Initially the connection at Tonbridge faced Ashford, as it was considered that the gradient would be too steep for a direct connection. Trains had to reverse to get to Tunbridge Wells. The junction at Tonbridge had the additional curve laid in by 1857. The land and works cost the railway £5,700.

The line from Tonbridge to Tunbridge Wells and on to Hastings was in marked contrast to the line to Dover. Due to the hilly nature of the High Weald, the line has steeper gradients and more curves and engineering works are required. It was this nature of the terrain and the haste with which the line was built which was to give it much of its character, some of which it retains to this day. The main problems are the tunnels, of which there are two between Tonbridge and Tunbridge Wells and a further four between Tunbridge Wells and Battle. Grove Hill Tunnel, immediately to the south of the station, was completed by March 1848 and Strawberry Hill Tunnel, which passes under Forest

Road, a few months later. By 1851 the works were well advanced and the board authorised expenditure on building five stations at Frant, Wadhurst, Witherenden renamed Ticehurst Road in December 1851 (later Stonegate). Etchingham and Robertsbridge. The station buildings were designed by London architect William Trees, and were among the most attractive built by the SER. The line was opened to Robertsbridge on 1st September 1851 with a special train to the Great Exhibition in London. The electric telegraph was installed from the outset and used for messages and regulating the train service. The section beyond Robertsbridge was delayed, due to poor ground conditions and weather delays. It finally opened to Hastings on 1st February 1852.

The Hastings line was built in a hurry and with what turned out to be a poor contractor. This was revealed in March 1855 when twelve feet of the Wadhurst tunnel collapsed, due to poor bricks being affected by frost and wet. An inspection of tunnels built by the same contractor was made and in Grove Hill Tunnel, the brickwork was tested by breaking through the crown of the roof. Only half-a-brick thickness was found, instead of the four brick thickness called for in the contract. It took several years for the resulting court case to be heard and in the meantime, the railway company had to make repairs at their own expense, as the contractor had gone bankrupt. Wadhurst and Mountfield tunnels also had to be relined, causing a restriction in the loading gauge which persisted until the tunnels were converted upon electrification to single line operation in 1986.

The Colebrook Viaduct at Southborough was the site of an early accident on the line in 1855. On 8th May 1855, locomotive no. 33 was travelling north with a Hastings to Tonbridge train which lost time at Tunbridge Wells while a large quantity of luggage was loaded into the guards van. The driver tried to make up time as he was three minutes late, and was travelling at 35 mph on the approach to the viaduct. The leading axle on the locomotive fractured and No. 33 left the track and turned over, killing the driver instantly and throwing the fireman into bushes which broke his fall and probably saved his life. Much of the train was derailed but remained upright, suffering little serious damage. The train consisted of one 2nd.class, one 1st.class and three 3rd. class coaches, plus the brake van. They would all have been four wheelers. (Early carriages were short [following stagecoach design] and had only four or six wheels per carriage. Later carriages would have two four-wheel bogies.)

One story from this period which is worth recounting is that the SER became involved in running special trains for persons, known as the 'Fancy' or the betting community, who wanted to attend illegal prize fights. It ran one to Edenbridge in 1850 for the fights of "Spider" Hailes v. Jem Madden and Wade v. Jones. Another was run in 1859 and again in 1860 to Etchingham. On 8th December 1863, the SER ran another special excursion to Wadhurst for a fight between King and Heenan. A train of 30 four- and six-wheel coaches and two locomotives conveying several hundred members of the 'Fancy' left London Bridge at 5:45 am. The police found out the match was to take place and turned up at Etchingham station to telegraph a message for reinforcements. The stationmaster told the police that they would have to wait their turn, as there were many messages to send. However, there did appear to have been time to telegraph the fight result to London.

The consequence of this was a summons to the SER to appear before the Sussex Eastern Sessions, where the SER had to agree that in future the police would be given priority of use on the telegraph, if requested. The SER had not done anything illegal in running a train to an illegal prize fight, but they ended up with a stern letter from the Home Secretary for their trouble. By 1868, Parliament included a clause in the Railway Bill outlawing the practice of running trains to prize fights.

The London, Brighton & South Coast Railway (LB&SCR) opened their line from East Grinstead to Tunbridge Wells West in 1866. It was an extension of the branch from Three Bridges to East Grinstead which had opened in 1855. The line was single track with stations at Forest Row, Hartfield, Withyham and Groombridge. Two years later, the line from Lewes to Uckfield which had been opened in 1858 was extended northwards as a single line, to join the East Grinstead to Tunbridge Wells line at Groombridge.

The biggest improvement to SER services from Tunbridge Wells came in 1869 when the new line to London via Sevenoaks was opened, shortening the route to the city by about twelve miles. This new shorter route to London by the SER was due mainly to the need to speed up the train service to London from Dover, due to the competition faced by the SER from its new rival, the London, Chatham & Dover Railway (LC&DR) which had opened to Victoria in 1862. From 1864, passengers could also get closer to the City and West End of London as Charing Cross and Cannon Street stations were opened that year. The LB&SCR was not a serious contender for the London traffic at this date as the route was slower and traffic from Tunbridge Wells had to run over a single line rural railway to Three Bridges until 1888, when the line through Oxted to Croydon was completed.

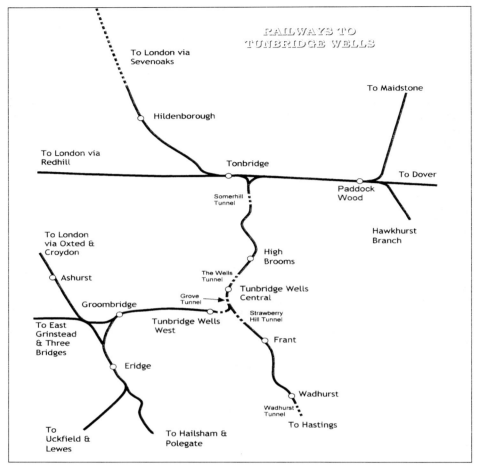

Schematic plan of railway connections between Tunbridge Wells and London, c.1900.

In 1872, the LB&SCR built a single line connection between the West and Central stations which initially was used only for the transfer of freight. A passenger service was started but only as a shuttle between the two stations. It would be some years before agreement would be reached about services of any distance across the company boundary. In 1880, the single line from Hailsham and Heathfield was extended northwards to join the Uckfield line at Eridge.

The next development happened in 1888 when the double-track line from Oxted to Ashurst Junction and Eridge was opened giving the Brighton company a shorter route to the capital than via Three Bridges. Finally, the line between Eridge and Lewes was doubled in 1894.

106

Tunbridge Wells had thus become a town with two stations operated by rival companies which serviced a network of lines radiating from the town. It was in the fortunate position of having the two stations close to the town centre, unlike many other stations in the Weald which were sometimes up to a couple of miles from the villages they purported to serve. But Tunbridge Wells to this day must be almost unique for a town of its size, in providing direct access to four London termini (Charing Cross, Waterloo, London Bridge and Cannon Street) and slightly less directly to Victoria (change at Redhill or East Croydon, although a direct service to Victoria from Tunbridge Wells was available until as recently as 2001).

The Tunbridge Wells Central Station in 1891. Note the siding on the left.

Facilities at the two stations were different. The SER Central station was built in a physically restricted area between two tunnels. In the early days there was room for some sidings, but these had to be accessed by turntables and so only short wagons could be accommodated. Some of these turntables can be seen in the print by J. C. Bourne which dates to the early 1850s. Coaches and wagons were moved on these turntables by manpower and accidents reported in the local press indicate that they were in use at least until 1856. Tunbridge Wells' main goods depot was on the site of the original station at Jackswood Springs, where there was more land available for coal yards, builders' merchants and the Baltic Saw Mills.

The LB & SCR station at Tunbridge Wells West was altogether a more splendid affair; and as it was built on what was at the time the edge of the town, there was more room and they built to impress. Tunbridge Wells West station also included a locomotive depot and carriage sidings to service the large network of rural railways radiating out to the western side of the town. (The depot and sidings are now the site of Sainsbury's and Homebase.)

The West, or Brighton, Station at Tunbridge Wells.

The railways served to bring visitors to the town and also to put Tunbridge Wells within commuting distance of London. The town thus started to develop rapidly in the mid-Victorian era. This led to development of housing and commercial life. One aspect of this growth is shown by the Gas Works, which by the 1870s had outgrown its town centre site in Golding Road. A new Gas Works was planned and opened alongside the railway in 1880 near the future site of High Brooms Station. In the early 1880s, the gas works was using between ten and twelve thousand tons of coal per annum to produce gas. By 1910-12, the annual consumption had risen to over 20,000 tons of coal and over 200,000 gallons of Gas oil. By-products from the gas works were coke, breeze, tar and Sulphate of ammonia. From 1899, the Tunbridge Wells gas works sold gas in bulk to Southborough UDC, who had a small gasholder of their own and their own network of mains. In 1895, the town started generation of electricity. Once again, the power station was built alongside the railway to make delivery of coal easy to handle.

Relations between the Town and the South Eastern Railway were never easy and early in 1878 the Courier reported that Mr. W. C. Cripps, solicitor to the Local Board (but later to be the first Town Clerk of the Borough of Tunbridge Wells) had placed a twelve-point case against the South Eastern Railway company to be heard by the Railway Commissioners, who were a body who could hear disputes between local parties and railway companies and give a binding verdict.

The Local Board's complaints noted that:
- the Down-side facilities were very poor. There was no access from the Up-side to the Down-side, other than by a long walk around the local roads, or a footpath across the top of the tunnel. Covered accommodation on the platforms was insufficient and the platforms were too short.
- Fares were complained about, as being too expensive and the railway reduced the first class single to London from 14s 6d to 13s. (£26 at 2005 prices, to £23)
- The Local Board wanted season ticket prices reduced, as Tunbridge Wells season ticket prices were the same as those from Hastings. They also wanted better connections with Redhill and improvements in 3rd class accommodation. They also wanted to keep third class fares from London to Tunbridge Wells high, so as to discourage the 'riff-raff.'

This action must have rattled the South Eastern because, a short while after, *The Courier* reports that agreement had been reached between the Local Board and the railway company about improvements to be made, without the case actually being heard by the Railway Commissioners.

Tunbridge Wells Central Station in 1878.

The improvements mentioned also included the new Grosvenor Bridge, to be built between the Upper Grosvenor Road and the St. James area of the town. In early June, *The Courier* reports work already started. The SER began a series of improvements. They installed a glazed roof over the Down-side platform and converted the old carriage shed into a waiting room. The covered footbridge was erected and the Up-side platform extended and the canopy rebuilt and extended.

Tunbridge Wells Local Board was still not happy with what had been done and an SER director was sent to look at the problem. In 1879, the SER bought up some houses to allow the improvement of the station. Extensions were made to the goods yard and new Signal boxes were provided between Tonbridge and Tunbridge Wells. In 1881, the sidings were further extended to allow for agricultural show traffic.

In the late 1880s, plans were brought forward for several schemes to provide another station in the area and finally in 1893, a station named Southborough was opened on 1st of March. This station was renamed High Brooms in 1925 to avoid confusion with the Southborough area of Bromley. In 1899, the South Eastern Railway entered a joint managing committee with the London, Chatham and Dover Railway. This formed the South Eastern & Chatham Railway.

Further developments were made to the Tunbridge Wells Central station in 1907 when the Vale Road bridge over the railway line was replaced with a wider bridge partly funded by the civic authorities. Following that, in 1912 the Down-side station buildings were redeveloped, to provide better facilities and a parade of shops, with offices above, facing Mount Pleasant.

From even before the First World War, the railway companies started to face competition for their freight traffic from motor lorries. The first traffic to suffer was the high value, time-critical produce which could now be taken straight from farm to London markets, without the multiple handling involved by taking it on the train. The return journeys could be used in bringing parcels of merchandise from wholesalers in London direct to Tunbridge Wells shops.

This process was hastened after the First World War, as in 1919 there was a prolonged strike, lasting several months, of railway staff who resented the reduction in wage rates that was imposed, following the end of the war and the easing of the labour shortage, which had pushed up wage rates during the war. This strike happened at just the time when there were many ex-army lorries available as government war surplus, and many men who had recently been demobilised, knew how to drive them. Many a small transport company started in the few years succeeding 1919. The Railways were in the position of being required to be general carriers by Parliament. Their rates of carriage were publicly known, so any enterprising lorry owner could undercut them. The railways increasingly were left with the bulk movement of fuel, coal and oil, and heavy low value long-distance freight such as stone for road making. As lorries improved, the railways lost further traffic, such as livestock and furniture removals.

Both the LBSCR and the SE&CR were amalgamated into the Southern Railway (SR) in 1923. The Southern Railway became the only one of the big four railways to derive more of its income from its (essentially commuting to London) passengers than freight.

Tunbridge Wells Central Station c.1900. Note siding at left.

The Southern Railway soon embarked on an ambitious modernisation programme which involved the extension of the electrification system in the suburban area and replacing outdated locomotives and coaches inherited from the former constituent companies. They provided new corridor trains in the late 1920s and more powerful 'Schools Class' locomotives in the 1930s. These locomotives and coaches had to be built specifically for the Hastings line as the restricted clearances in the tunnels prevented two trains passing in safety, if each were more than eight feet wide. *The Courier* for December 1953 recorded complaints from Tunbridge Wells to London commuters that the early morning trains were overcrowded and had little improved since 1928. These 1928 built trains however had to last well into the British Railways era.

The sidings at the Central Station were removed in about 1928 and the platforms were lengthened to accommodate the new longer coaches, and the signal box was removed, with its functions being replaced by those at Grove Junction and Tunbridge Wells Goods signal boxes. Once the two rival companies were put under the same administration, more use was made of the link between the Central and West stations. This allowed coaching stock to be berthed and locomotives serviced away from the main Tonbridge to Hastings line where there was no room for sidings. The Southern Railway became the Southern Region of the newly nationalised British Railways on the 1st January 1948.

One of the results of the British Railways modernisation plan of 1955 was the intention to convert to diesel or electric operation. In the case of the Tonbridge to Hastings line, it was decided to build a fleet of narrow diesel electric trains that would be able to run through the restricted tunnels on the line. These entered service in 1957 and remained in operation until 1986. One of these trains survives in preservation, based at Hastings, and is hired out for emergency cover for failed units on the Hastings to Ashford line, or for special excursions. Being a narrow unit that is self powered, it can travel anywhere on the UK rail system and has travelled more widely, since it left main line service.

As part of the so-called Beeching rationalisation of the railway network, many of the lines built by the former LB&SCR were closed in the 1960s. The only line to remain is the Oxted to Uckfield via Eridge and Crowborough, but this was reduced from double to single track. The last section to close entirely was Tunbridge Wells to Eridge which closed in 1985, partly as a consequence of the work done to electrify the main line to Hastings. Part of the Tunbridge Wells to Eridge line currently is used by the Spa Valley Railway.

By the early 1980s, the diesel trains introduced in 1957 were in their turn starting to show signs of increasing age and thoughts turned to how it would be possible to electrify the line and use standard width electric multiple units that had been in use in the rest of southern England since the mid 1960s. It was no longer economically viable to build a small fleet of narrow trains just for the route through Tunbridge Wells. It was decided that as the Bournemouth line was to have new rolling stock, there would be sufficient displaced electric units available to run the service to Hastings which, combined with installing a single, reversible, line of track in the narrow tunnels, and installing only sufficient power supply to operate four coach trains south of Tunbridge Wells, the project would be economically viable. So in 1986, the Tonbridge to Hastings line was electrified and several of the tunnels converted to single reversible track to allow the use of standard width electric multiple slam-door units. The timetable was adjusted so that in normal service, trains would not be needing to pass each other where there was a single line section.

Following accidents elsewhere, it was recommended that the slam door units be replaced, but they have taken a long time to go and there are a few left still running in June 2005 which makes them about forty years old. Within the last couple of years, new class '375' electric trains have replaced those that were running on our line since 1986. These now have the luxury of power operated sliding doors and air-conditioning. However the seating is more in common with economy class on the airlines. The introduction of these has not been without problems as the electrification in 1986 was done on the cheap. The new trains use more electricity and so an enhanced electricity supply has had to be installed before full length trains could be run.

Even today the relationship between the Town and the Railway is still poor, with complaints and meetings between the railway management and our town officials and MP featuring on a regular basis in the local press. People seem to look back and think that there was a 'Golden Age', but it is doubtful if it ever existed. It seems that the railway will never satisfy the good burghers of Tunbridge Wells. Let's face it, they've been grumbling about it for over a hundred years. Why should they stop now?

Sketch of bridge over railway at Tunbridge Wells c.1851.
The buildings over the bridge are the site today of Hoopers.

CHAPTER 10

CANON HOARE
AND THE VICTORIAN ECCLESIASTICAL SCENE

by Geoffrey Copus

Seventeenth and eighteenth century Tunbridge Wells had a well-deserved reputation as a resort for the frivolous, peopled during the season largely by pleasure-seekers of the upper classes. The Anglican chapel of ease with the splendidly church-and-state dedication in honour of King Charles the Martyr was opened in 1678, enlarged in 1682 and doubled in size in the 1690s. Until Ewan Christian's restoration of 1882, it had the appearance of a preaching-house, with galleries around three sides of the building. Christian added a short chancel in suitable classical style, and left the church appearing very much as it does today. It retains a strong seventeenth century atmosphere, a calm oasis amidst the constant rush of traffic uncomfortably close by.

As well as King Charles' chapel, there was from the first a considerable Nonconformist presence. The Baptists were active in the area from early in the seventeenth century, followed by the Presbyterians who met at Mount Ephraim House from 1689. John Wesley paid a number of visits to Tunbridge Wells, where the Methodists were established from about 1762.

Emannuel Church

One of the missions of Selina, Countess of Huntingdon, "the Apostle to the upper classes", (1707-1791) was to open places of worship "especially in watering places where people congregated at different time of the year"[1] including Bath, Margate and Cheltenham. Tunbridge Wells was an obvious choice, and here a "little wooden sanctuary" was built on Mount Ephraim, and opened in 1769. The chapel prospered, and the humble building, known as Emmanuel, was extended several times before being replaced in 1867 by a fine new Gothic style church with a needle spire 140 feet high, designed by Wimble and Taylor, and a major landmark in Tunbridge Wells. Alas, the Connexion

Holy Trinity Church, c.1830.

and the local congregation dwindled and, despite protest, the building was demolished in 1974 to extend the forecourt of the adjacent Kent and Sussex Hospital and provide access to its lower car park. Only a part of the churchyard remains, with the monument to mark the spot where the celebrated George Whitefield had stood to preach at the opening of the original chapel.

The Church of England presence was not extended further until the development of the Calverley estate began. In 1827, a little before any of the houses were built, the foundation stone of Holy Trinity church was laid on the birthday of the Duchess of Kent, Queen Victoria's mother. Decimus Burton, the estate's architect, also designed the church.

In a separate initiative, Christ Church in the High Street was begun in 1835, to cater for the inhabitants of the development of houses which had begun to creep up the hill, although it would be some time before the old and new parts of the town would meet. Both

Christ Church.

these churches were old-fashioned for their period, not unlike eighteenth century preaching houses, but whereas Holy Trinity was designed in a Gothic style, Christ Church (sadly now no more) was externally at least distinctive, with a prominent neo-Norman tower.

Canon Edward Hoare.

It was in 1853 that the Rev. Edward Hoare (always remembered as Canon Hoare, an honour bestowed on him in 1868) was presented to Holy Trinity, beginning an incumbency of some 40 years during which his influence on Tunbridge Wells was immense. Hoare had been born into a wealthy Quaker family; Samuel Hoare his father was a City banker, while his mother was a sister of Elizabeth Fry, the inspirational prison reformer. His parents had been received into the Church as adults, and he himself was not baptised until the age of 15 since, as Edward wrote "my father never completely lost his early Quaker prejudice against infant baptism."[2] In view of the Quaker tradition of tolerance, it is perhaps strange that Edward, influenced by his upbringing in strict Evangelical principles, was so aggressively opposed to any other views in the increasingly diverse Church of England.

Hoare came to Tunbridge Wells from Christ Church, Ramsgate, which he had built, and where his memory is still revered. Where many of the new generation of Victorian clergy would have chafed at the bleak "Gothick" interior of Holy Trinity, Edward Hoare was delighted with the practical aspects of the building, which he described as "an excellent church, which, though I do not suppose it would satisfy the ecclesiologist, I have found to be most commodious for the worship of God. There are three things in it quite at variance with modern fashion: instead of an open roof to generate cold in winter, heat in summer, and echo at all times, we have had a flat ceiling to protect us from all changes of the climate; and instead of having the people spread far and wide on the ground floor, there are deep galleries along three sides of the church, containing nearly six hundred persons, all within ear-shot; and instead of a low pulpit scarcely raising the preacher above the heads of his hearers, there is an old-fashioned "three-decker" of sufficient height to enable the preacher to see the whole of his congregation."

The parish of Holy Trinity was initially a large one, which became increasingly unwieldy with the growth of population in the town. To meet this development, Canon Hoare was instrumental in building the

daughter churches of St. John's, St. John's Road (1858); St James's, St. James's Road (1860-62); and St. Peter's, Bayhall Road (1874-75).

St. John's was originally designed by Alexander Dick Gough of London, but considerably altered later in the

Evangelical simplicity – the interior of Holy Trinity Church in late Victorian times.

St. James'.

nineteenth century by the local firm of architects, Henry Hickman Cronk and Egbert Cronk. They it was, who removed the original short spire and, taking advantage of the prominent site, built instead the fine Kentish-style western tower.

The distinguished Ewan Christian, the Canterbury Diocesan Architect, and later President of the Royal Institute of British Architects, designed St. James's, and perhaps the Vicarage next door – now Church House. A notable feature of the church's interior is the marble font consisting of an angel holding a shell, copied from Thorwaldson's design of 1823. The tall spire and the rural setting of the church in its greensward churchyard is most attractive.

St. Peter's.

St. Peter's was designed by Henry Hickman Cronk, (who incidentally was a Churchwarden of Holy Trinity) and the north aisle was added in 1889. The fine spire is a prominent landmark, and the tower has the only ring of 8 bells in the town. It is recorded of the Rev. Charles Courtenay, Vicar from 1895 to 1912[3] that he decided that his family should sit at the back during services so that Mrs. Courtenay could note the size and nature of the congregation. No tradesman could hope for the Vicarage patronage unless he was a member of St. Peter's, and if he was not in Church on Sunday, his absence would be commented on when he called for his orders during the following week – an illustration of the influence to conform, exerted on Victorian citizens of the town.

Happily, these three churches established through the initiative of Canon Hoare survive and flourish to this day, and within the Evangelical tradition. There was however a period of fierce strife in the early history of St. James's which led to the creation of the parish of St. Barnabas.

Canon Hoare naturally appointed the first Vicar of St. James's, and chose the Rev. Christopher Ridley Pearson, the son of his predecessor at Holy Trinity and therefore thought to be a safe pair of hands to maintain the Evangelical tradition. To Canon Hoare's horror, Mr. Pearson, influenced like many of the younger generation of clergy by the Tractarian movement, began to introduce mildly "high church" practices. In a memorable phrase Alan Savidge wrote[4] that these "would

High Church exuberance – the altar of St. Stephen's, built 1870, demolished 1887.

raise few eyebrows nowadays" but to Canon Hoare and like-minded inhabitants of the new parish they were deeply offensive. The building of the Mission Church of St. Stephen in Stanley Road in 1870, and the arrival of Anglican nuns to look after children in an orphanage nearby, caused more outrage.

This was a long and involved saga, but despite Canon Hoare's opposition Mr. Pearson gained the support of the Archbishop of Canterbury (in whose Diocese Tunbridge Wells then lay) and was able to establish St. Barnabas' parish in 1881. This task accomplished, he resigned from St. James's, which returned to Canon Hoare's fold.

Interior, St. Barnabas.

The present church of St. Barnabas was built on the site of St. Stephen's in 1887-8 and is of brick, on a cathedral-like scale. The architects were the brothers J.E.K. and J.P. Cutts, who designed numbers of somewhat similar, distinctively "town" churches. Alone among the churches of Tunbridge Wells, St. Barnabas' has sumptuous fittings, including among much else an iron screen with a crucifix and attendant figures by Harry Hems, a statue and a banner designed by Sir Ninian Comper, and chapels in both Italianate and Gothic style by Martin Travers.

*St. Mark's,
Broadwater Down.*

Outside Canon Hoare's formal influence, since it was originally in the Diocese of Chichester, was St. Mark's, Broadwater Down of 1864-66, the cost of which was borne by the Earl of Abergavenny whose estate in the southern part of the town was then being developed. The architect was Robert Louis Roumieu, and the building, of local stone, shows evidence of his highly personal style, the slender spire widely visible on the Tunbridge Wells skyline.

St. Paul's, Rusthall.

Also outside Canon Hoare's influence was St. Paul's, Rusthall, built by the exertions of the Rev. J. J. Saint, Rector of Speldhurst, and originally consisting only of a nave and chancel, with a lofty central tower. The architect was Henry Isaac Stevens of Derby, who presumably obtained the commission through his brother, the obscure Tunbridge Wells architect Nehemiah Edward Stevens, who is credited with having had a minor role at St. Paul's.

The building was enlarged in 1864 by the addition of a north aisle, and again in 1913 by one bay westwards, a large western narthex and baptistery. Several well-known artists have contributed to the enrichment of the building, including Sir Walter Tapper, Martin Travers and Sir Edward Burne-Jones. The elaborate carved stone reredos was presented to the church in 1867 and incurred the wrath of one of the parishioners, the Rev. T. Jennings Bramly of Nevill Park, who bombarded the Archbishop[5] in an unsuccessful endeavour to have it removed as being "Popish."

The gusto with which Victorians like this indulged in religious controversy in Tunbridge Wells can best be appreciated by a study of the local press. Apart from tediously lengthy correspondence, there were detailed reports of excitements which seem to have been much enjoyed by the rowdy

St. Augustine's Roman Catholic Church c. 1840.

element of the town. A lady called Edith O'Gorman, the self-styled "escaped nun", stirred up a good deal of anti-Catholic feeling at a public meeting sponsored by the Vicar of Christ Church, with the squabbling factions in the audience firmly restrained by the local police force.

The Roman Catholic church of St. Augustine's had been opened in 1838; an attractive classical building by Joseph Ireland with an impressive later tower, it formed part of a Catholic enclave together with the school and the Presbytery. For understandable reasons, all have now been swept away and the church and presbytery rebuilt in Crescent Road, with the schools on larger sites further north, but the passing of such an attractive group can only be regretted.

The modest red brick Hanover Strict Baptist chapel nearby, built in 1833, has happily survived, close to the Baptist church in Upper Grosvenor Road, an ambitious and successful work of 1938 by C.H. Strange with an attractive tower.

Among other Nonconformist places of worship which have survived in use are the charming Friends' Meeting House of 1894 in Grosvenor Park

Hanover Chapel.

and, nearby, what is now the United Reformed church. The latter, with integral manse, was designed by the local architect Herbert Murkin Caley, and built (as St. John's Free church) for the Rev. James Mountain, a fiery local preacher who had seceded from the Countess of Huntingdon's Connexion. The Methodist church, of 1872, by Charles Bell of London, in a prominent position in Vale Road, was well adapted to modern needs after being reprieved from possible demolition. The United Reformed church at Hawkenbury (1889, by Potts, Sulman and Hennings) is an early

United Reformed Church at Hawkenbury c. 1900.

and successful example of a complex of buildings to cater for many different activities.

The York Road Meeting House is a modest but most attractive late 19th. century building with classical detailing ex- ternally. The Church of Christ, Commercial Road, built as the Christians Meeting

Congregational Church in Mount Pleasant c. 1850.

House in 1877, is another attractive little building of light-coloured brick with stone dressings.

Among Nonconformist buildings now converted to secular use, the former Congregational church in Mount Pleasant (now a Habitat shop) is the most notable. This may have been designed by Jabez Scholes, the stonemason who built it in 1848. If so, he did a considerable service to the town by providing such a handsome building on a prominent site, looking very much like a classical temple.

Canon Hoare is shown at his most intransigent in the controversy over St. Barnabas, and as may be seen from his biography he was also an implacable enemy of the Roman Catholics, but he enjoyed a warm relationship with the Protestant Nonconformists. His huge reputation as a preacher drew great crowds to hear him at Holy Trinity, justifying the contemporary comment that "here (as in many other towns) the congregational system has long since to all intents and purposes superseded the parochial."[6]

Canon Hoare had many supporters among the wealthy inhabitants of the district, particularly the Deacon family of Mabledon at Tonbridge. The formidable Archbishop Benson wrote in his private diary in May 1883:

"On Saturday went to Tunbridge Wells and confirmed 400 people in Canon Hoare's church... Most interesting confirmation in the very Beulah of these darling old Evangelicals. We stayed most happily with the Deacons in their beautiful home... meeting the Evangelical Shepherds and Sheep, for Mr. Deacon suffers none beside. They are all right – they hold nothing but the truth and they hold it strongly, consistently, sweetly, but with just a little tinge of Torquemada... There is something in Evangelicism, as it exists now, in "Protestant truth," as dear Mr. Deacon calls it, which is very concordant with wealth."[7]

In the increasingly secular society of the twenty-first century, it is difficult to comprehend the hold which Canon Hoare had on attitudes in Tunbridge Wells. It is ironic too that his own church should have narrowly survived efforts by one of his successors to have it demolished, along with Christ Church and two Methodist churches, to make way for a joint Anglican/Methodist building on the site. This frenzy of destruction was fortunately frustrated, largely through the efforts of the Civic Society.

Canon Hoare's biography recounts the tale of of one gentleman asking another "How is it that you have no theatre at Tunbridge Wells ? ..."Oh", responded his companion, "it would never pay. Tunbridge Wells is too religious a place for a theatre." This adds credence to the local legend that when a theatre did come to be built in the town, some years after Canon Hoare's death, it was called The Opera House in deference to his continuing influence. What would Canon Hoare think if he revisited his old church today, to find it operating as a highly successful Arts Centre, a conversion aided by the features of the original design that he had found so praiseworthy?

The picture so far given of Canon Hoare is somewhat unsympathetic, and should be balanced by stressing the other, warmer side of his character. Undoubtedly influenced by his Quaker origins, he did a great deal for the bodies as well as the souls of the poor of his parish, and those who passed through it. He operated Mission Services, temperance meetings and soup kitchens very much on the lines adopted by the Salvation Army but, as he put it, "without the aid of a fiddle or a flag." His warm relationship with his children and grandchildren also comes out strongly in his letters to them. His biographer wrote of Canon Hoare's death:

"It is impossible to describe the feeling exhibited in Tunbridge Wells when it was known that Canon Hoare had passed away, and on the day of the funeral the town witnessed such a display of universal sorrow and respect as it had never seen before... It is enough to say that everything which could be done by the Mayor and Corporation and inhabitants of the town to declare their loss and emphasise their respect was done. More than one Bishop and over a hundred clergy walked in the ranks of the mourners... A little book published at this time contains in full all that was said and done with reference to him who had passed away... the funeral sermons preached all over the town, in church and chapel alike.."[2]

A monument to Canon Hoare with portrait bust, designed by John Oldrid Scott, was erected near St. John's Church – an unusual tribute, which narrowly escaped destruction when threatened by road-widening. Here again, the Civic Society mounted a spirited protest, as a result of which the Borough Council re-sited the monument nearby, where it remains as a tribute to a truly Great Man, of a type which, it would seem, has long since died out.

Canon Hoare Memorial. Junction of St. John's Road and Culverden Park.

CHAPTER 11

FIGHTING FOR THE FUTURE

by Ian Beavis

Ever since the decline of its popularity as a fashionable spa resort, Tunbridge Wells had been trying to make up its mind whether it wanted to become a lively, prosperous and innovative town, or a quiet rural backwater. Even the developer John Ward, whom we may now see as saving Tunbridge Wells from fading into the obscurity of a minor Wealden village, was criticised by many of his contemporaries who saw him destroying forever the rustic informality of the old settlement centred on the Pantiles. Earlier still, Benge Burr in his 1766 History of Tunbridge Wells had advocated new developments to compete with Brighton, while attacking those 'men of narrow souls and short-sighted views' who were opposed to such radical change.

In the 1880s, these opposing viewpoints were focussed on the debate over incorporation, the great question being whether the old Local Board was sufficient local government to meet the town's foreseeable needs, or whether a stronger and more prestigious borough council was needed to take the town forward into a new era. Supporters of incorporation could argue that Tunbridge Wells was already a radically different place from what it had been when the town's first local government was instituted.

As early as 1871, Pelton's Guide was able to say that 'Tunbridge Wells has undergone a great change within the memory of the elder among its inhabitants and frequenters. Up to within a very recent period, it was strictly a watering place; it was visited during a few months of the year by those who came to drink the chalybeate waters for the benefit of their health, and by those who were attracted by its air, scenery, society and gaieties. But during the last forty years, especially during the latter half of that period, the town has become a very favourite place of residence, and families of wealth and leisure, with no strong local attachments elsewhere, have selected it as their abode'.

Spearheaded by groups like the Tradesmen's Association, who were in the forefront of every movement to modernise and improve Tunbridge Wells, the campaign to renew the town's local government was pursued vigorously. One of the leading opponents of incorporation was John Stone-Wigg, who had served as Chairman of the Local Board since 1878 and was a staunch defender of the existing system, fearing that 'a Corporation was often synonymous with corruption.' However, in 1888,

27th February 1889: W. C. Cripps, the first Town Clerk, reading the new Borough Charter.

as his obituary relates, 'reading the Times over the breakfast table, he came to the conclusion from Mr Ritchie's speech in the House of Commons in introducing the Local Government Bill, that the new county authority to be set up might interfere with the independence of the town if it were not a municipality.' His was one voice that could not be ignored, and he was shortly able to lead the Board in a complete reversal of its previous policy. The Board voted to petition the Privy Council for a charter, the subsequent government enquiry approved the request, and the petition was granted on 16 January 1889. The deputation sent to collect the charter on 27 February brought it proudly back by special train to the West Station, where its arrival was greeted by a 21-gun salute fired from the Common opposite. A 'Grand Procession' then escorted the charter deputation to the town hall through streets decorated with flags and triumphal arches.

Alderman John Stone-Wigg, the first Mayor of Tunbridge Wells, 1889-91.

Under the new constitution, four wards would in future elect six councillors each for three year terms, and there would be eight aldermen elected by the council for six years. John Stone-Wigg became the first mayor, serving from 1889 to 1891.

He paid the legal costs of obtaining the charter, arranged the design of armorial bearings for the new authority, and presented the mayoral chain of office. The mace was presented in 1891 by Aldermen Hori Pink (the borough's second mayor) and Philip Jackson.

W. C. Cripps.

Curiously enough, the new Borough Council was rarely called by that name: in popular parlance and in official publications, it was usually the Town Council, or the Tunbridge Wells Corporation. The powers of the new local authority were set out in the Tunbridge Wells Improvement Act of 1890. The successful passage through Parliament of this very detailed and comprehensive piece of legislation, despite opposition from some quarters, was attributed by contemporaries to the skill of the first Town Clerk, William Charles Cripps, son of a former Commissioner and local solicitor who set up the practice which is today Cripps, Harries Hall. He was a local solicitor who became Clerk to the Improvement Commissioners in 1887, and then the first Town Clerk, not retiring until 1925.

Politics in the new borough (as in nearly all boroughs of the time) was not run on national party lines, but according to local issues. Councillors tended to fall into two not always clearly defined camps, representing the pre-existing divergence of opinion about where the town's best interests lay. The 'progressive' party, as they were generally known, wanted to keep up the momentum of modernisation, supported by pressure groups like the Tradesmen's Association and the Improvement Association. The progressives favoured expenditure on ambitious public works as an investment in the town's future prosperity, and they supported the direct provision of public utilities by the Council – a policy which their opponents condemned as 'municipal trading'. Those opponents, who are less often named but sometimes styled themselves the 'moderate' party, favoured low rates and minimal intervention by the Council, preferring to see public services provided by private enterprise. Two rival newspapers, *The Advertiser* and *The Courier*, offered support to the progressives and their opponents respectively, making no secret of their political affiliations and helping to promote a culture of vigorous public debate.

In the late Victorian period, the progressive party was in the ascendant, the high point of their influence being the year 1894-5 when Sir David

Salomons, though not a councillor, was asked to serve as mayor. *The Advertiser's* souvenir supplement made no secret of the fact that Gilbert Finch, the Council's original nominee, had been pressurised by public opinion into stepping aside in favour of this more prestigious candidate.

Accepting the invitation, Sir David presided over a year in which Tunbridge Wells found itself unexpectedly propelled to the forefront of modern technology. 'No one,' reported *The Sketch*, 'has done so much as the present mayor to infuse into the sleepy hollow of this most charming Kentish inland watering-place the life-blood of the latest scientific improvements, and this has had the inevitable effect of putting the town in the forefront of popular observation.' On mayor-making day, there was a procession headed by the police and the Ceylon Band through streets decorated with flags and bunting to a luncheon at the Pump Room. The local MP, Arthur Boscawen, made a speech in which the leading party's watchword was prominently featured. 'Tunbridge Wells' he

Sir David Lionel Salomons Bt.

declared 'had a great future before it. The town, which possessed great natural advantages, had risen very rapidly. He was told that, during Sir David's mayoralty, it would take the first position of all fashionable resorts. There were many things which the inhabitants had set their hearts upon, and he hoped to see them accomplished very soon. He felt certain that in Sir David Salomons they would have a Mayor who would favour every progressive policy for the benefit of Tunbridge Wells.'

Sir David Salomons is best remembered today as a pioneer of the motor car. Feeling that Britain was lagging behind in embracing this new invention and seeking to promote a wider understanding of the possibilities that it offered, he organised Britain's first motor show at the Agricultural Showground off the Eridge Road on 15 October 1895. The show was attended by some eight thousand people, including visitors from America, France, Germany and several other countries. At the end of the day, Sir David announced that he would offer a further demonstration by driving his own vehicle up and down the Eridge Road. This was strictly in defiance of the 'Red Flag Act' of 1865 which placed great restrictions on the use of motor vehicles on public highways, but as the borough had its own police force, this was not going to be enforced. Sir David's campaign to repeal the Act was in any case nearing its successful conclusion.

15th October 1895. First Motor Show in Britain, at Tunbridge Wells.

The press had mixed feelings about the potential of this startling new technology. The local *Courier* proved quite visionary, posing the question 'Will the horses of the future be fed upon petroleum instead of oats?' The report continued by saying that 'Those who observed the facile celerity with which Sir David's elegant carriage, propelled by an unseen motor, moved round the show ring must be impressed with the fact that we are on the eve of a great revolution in our means of highway locomotion. France has been allowed to get ahead of us, which is not a credit to an engineering nation like our own, and with the unknown possibilities of a new industry being opened up in this country, it is no small honour to Tunbridge Wells that it should be associated with the first organised attempt to give the horseless carriage a standing in this country.'

Some of the national press agreed, the *Daily Chronicle* looking forward to a day when 'the elderly ladies of Tunbridge Wells will steer themselves to church in bath-chairs that go of themselves', adding that 'Time has still in reserve some wonders for the end of the century.' *The Daily Telegraph*, on the other hand, was much less enthusiastic. Answering the rhetorical question 'Will these things come into vogue?', it confidently predicted:

'That the petroleum motor will ever supersede the pleasure horse is in the highest degree unlikely. That London Society will pay its calls, and go to dinners, dances, or the theatre in a private horseless carriage is perhaps not a state of things which is yet within measurable distance.'

On 9 October 1895, just a few days before the motor show, Sir David inaugurated the town's first electricity supply system, introducing another of the several technologies which he had helped to pioneer. The national press took a great interest. The *Daily News* said that 'People who imagine the Wells, the Pantiles and all the pleasant surroundings of this noted resort to have become old-fashioned and out-of-date would have been agreeably surprised to see yesterday's installation of the most modern illuminant. Through the enterprise of the Town Council, headed by Sir David Salomons, the community has embarked on an expenditure of £25,000 to render their good old town more agreeable to visitors at night and also more useful to themselves.'

At a reception hosted by Sir David at the Friendly Societies' Hall in Camden Road, guests were entertained by tales of the opposition that was encountered when the prospect of mains electricity was first raised. One lady had written to the Council declaring that 'she would not have an

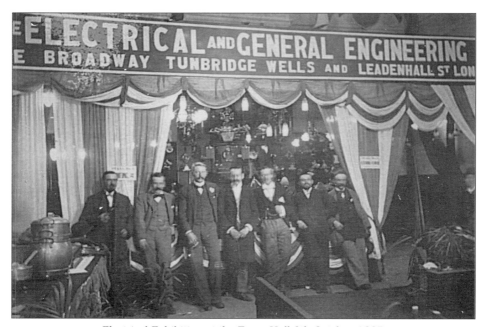

Electrical Exhibition at the Town Hall 9th October, 1895.

electric lamp in her house if it was supplied for nothing, and that the lights which it was proposed to erect in the roadways would be certain to wither the trees.'

Following the reception, the guests proceeded through decorated streets to the new generating station near the Grosvenor Bridge, where Lady Laura Salomons switched on the power. 'Subsequently', *The Morning Post* related, 'a procession of police, military, firemen, local clubs, the tradesmen's association, officials and members of the Corporation, the Mayor and Mayoress, escorted by the Yeomanry, and in which Sir David Salomons' petroleum carriage was a conspicuous object, paraded the streets as far as the Town Hall.' There an exhibition had been set up to demonstrate to a perhaps still sceptical public the possibilities of the new technology. As *The Daily Telegraph* explained, 'It is obviously desirable that when the electric light is put at the service of a locality for the first time its inhabitants should be able to see for themselves how efficiently it can be adapted to domestic use; and a display of cosy boudoirs, elegantly illuminated by the softest of electric lights, or of dinner tables rendered brilliant by the introduction of electric candelabra, is calculated to somewhat open the eyes of the average gas consumer.'

Much of the appeal of Victorian Tunbridge Wells to visitors and potential residents lay in its open spaces, the most notable of which were Tunbridge Wells and Rusthall Commons. As Pelton's Guide famously declared, 'What the ocean is to a sea-bathing town, that the Common is to Tunbridge Wells.' The appropriateness of the seaside analogy can be seen from the Mount Ephraim 'Promenade' of 1881-91, as well as those numerous postcard views entitled Sunday Afternoon on the Common which depict crowds sitting on the grassy slopes overlooking London Road or around the Wellington Rocks.

Throughout most of the nineteenth century, the Commons, owned by the Manor of Rusthall, had been managed by the Freeholders, local residents with traditional grazing and other rights. The Local Board had wished for some time to gain more control over the Commons, especially after their impotence was made humiliatingly clear in the affair of the enclosure of St Helena Cottage in the early 1880s. This threat to the integrity of the Commons was overcome only through the enterprise of Frank William Stone, later mayor, who managed to pack the Freeholders' Committee with his supporters.

Control over the Commons was one of the many issues dealt with under the Tunbridge Wells Improvement Act of 1890. The parliamentary process was originally set in motion by the Local Board prior to Incorporation. The Manor and the Freeholders, who felt that they had looked after the Commons perfectly satisfactorily since time immemorial, objected to the Board's ambitions and petitioned parliament in opposition to the original version of the Bill. Negotiations were opened between the three parties, and the compromise that eventually featured in the Act established a body, known as the Conservators, to manage the Commons. This body was to consist of four representatives appointed by the Manor, the Freeholders and the new Borough Council, with a duty to 'maintain the Commons free from all encroachments.' The Act also stated explicitly for the first time that 'the inhabitants of Tunbridge Wells and the neighbourhood shall have free access.'

The Grove, Mount Sion, c.1900.

Another, much smaller, open space featured in the Improvement Act was the Grove on Mount Sion. Until that time, the management of the Grove had remained in the hands of the body of trustees established when the self-styled Earl of Bucking-ham donated it as a local amenity in 1703. Many improvements had been carried out under the direction of William Law Pope, the public-spirited minister of King Charles' Church, who was the leading trustee from 1864 and was styled as Honorary Curator of the Grove. The 1890 Act transferred the Grove to the newly established Borough Council under the provisions of the original trust, with minor variations. The Council enthusiastically set about embellishing the Grove, adding iron railings, ornamental gates, seats, lamp standards and a bandstand.

The town's first purpose-made municipal park was Grosvenor Recreation Ground. Part of the land now occupied by the park was the site of the original town waterworks, fed by Jackswood Spring. In 1885 John Stone-Wigg, chairman of the Local Board, offered to present to the town four acres of land adjacent to the old waterworks and refuse tip, on condition that the whole area be converted into a public recreation ground. His wish was to provide a recreational area for the northern part of the town which did not have the benefit of the Commons as an open space. In later years an eyewitness recalled how 'the Town Commissioners went to inspect the site, and their proceedings were curiously watched by a group of urchins looking through the Auckland Road entrance to the town dust heap. Mr Stone-Wigg caught sight of them and exclaimed "Here, gentlemen, are our petitioners". The effect was electrical, and the East End children's playground soon became an accomplished fact.'

The Board commissioned a plan for the development of the park from the distinguished landscape designer Robert Marnock, who at a much

earlier stage in his career had created the then private Dunorlan Park. Work on the new recreation ground proceeded through 1888 to the first half of 1889. Ornamental lakes, fed by springs, were created, the largest being embellished with an island and a row of 'dripping wells' or 'grottoes'.

Grosvenor Recreation Ground, c.1900.

With his interest in providing open spaces for healthy recreation, John Stone-Wigg was also concerned for the needs of the expanding St John's area. At the time of his death, he was planning to purchase some land for this purpose. It was appropriate therefore that his children should have decided to finance the purchase of the town's second recreation ground in his memory. In the autumn of 1899, some meadow land belonging to Down Farm was acquired, and over the next few months paths and tennis courts were laid out, trees and shrubs planted, and seats provided. The St John's Recreation Ground was formally opened on 13 June 1900.

There had long been talk of a third recreation ground, making use of the park that originally served Decimus Burton's Calverley Hotel. The hotel grounds consisted of meadows with a scattering of trees and a lake at their lowest point. The acquisition of the park and its development into a public garden and recreation ground was considered as early as 1864, when private enterprise proposed a summer and winter gardens and aquarium, with an entrance opposite the station.

In 1894 the Tradesmen's Association lobbied the Council to acquire the park for a summer and winter garden, but in the following year attention was diverted to the possibility of a public pleasure garden at the Pantiles end of Warwick Park. This failed to come to fruition, and by 1911 both the Council and Tradesmen's Association were agreed on a policy of acquiring the Calverley site. Negotiations were opened with the Calverley Estate, but came to nothing. However, the purchase of the park and the Great Hall was finally achieved in 1921, enabling the creation of today's Calverley Grounds.

In the late nineteenth and early twentieth centuries, band concerts were hugely popular among visitors and residents. A band of local musicians performing around the town is mentioned in guide books as early as 1839, and continued in one form or another throughout the Victorian era. However, there were criticisms of the quality of its performances, and in 1896 the newly formed Borough Band Committee decided to take control of public music by appointing a professional bandmaster. They chose Matthew Marks of the Royal Marine Band in Portsmouth and gave him the task of forming a new Borough Band which would provide the high profile daily concerts on the Pantiles, as well as a regular programme of performances at other venues such as the Common, Grosvenor Recreation Ground and the Grove. 'Tunbridge Wells has a band', wrote the *Eastbourne Gazette*, 'and they don't forget to let you

The Tunbridge Wells Borough Band, also known as the Ceylon Band.

133

know it either. The men are uniformed in gorgeous red and white tunics, black trousers with white stripes, and smart red and white caps, à la Francais.' Audiences of well over a thousand were regularly attracted.

The first covered bandstand was installed in 1897 in the Grove. It was at the centre of an illuminated concert to celebrate Queen Victoria's Diamond Jubilee, which featured elaborate decorations with seven thousand coloured lamps and Chinese lanterns and was described as 'almost Parisian in variety, beauty and extent.' In 1899 Councillor Elvy Robb presented a second bandstand to be installed in Grosvenor Recreation Ground. For many years, since Victorian bands had outgrown the accommodation provided by the Music Gallery, performers on the Pantiles had at best a simple wooden platform, with the option of using the Pump Room if it rained. This inconvenience was finally remedied in September 1900 when the new Pantiles bandstand was opened. The final and most ambitious provisions for the band season were the ornate bandstand and pavilion constructed in Calverley Grounds between 1924 and 1926 but severely damaged by enemy action during World War II.

Charles Fletcher Lutwidge.

The progressive party in local politics continued its ascendancy under Sir David Salomons' successor, Major Charles Fletcher Lutwidge, cousin of Lewis Carroll (Charles Lutwidge Dodgson). He served as mayor from 1895 to 1898, and again in 1901-2. Efforts had been made to persuade Sir David to continue in office. When he declined, it proved difficult to find anyone willing to follow him, as his mayoral year had been so spectacular. Eventually another figure from outside the Council had to be persuaded to fill the gap. The *Courier* graphically describes Lutwidge's initial reluctance: 'In vain he protested that he knew nothing of local administration. His hesitation had to yield to a numerously and influentially signed memorial.'

The high point of Lutwidge's mayoralty was perhaps the Diamond Jubilee year of 1897, during which he laid the foundation stone of the Indoor Swimming Bath in Monson Road. This was a facility that had long been campaigned for by the Cygnus Swimming Club, as a cold weather alternative to the old open air bath at Grosvenor Recreation Ground. He was remembered too for providing lavish public entertainments, including Jubilee celebrations in the grounds of the Great Hall, which were attended by some nine thousand people.

Other public institutions which Fletcher Lutwidge supported included the Technical Institute opened in Monson Road in 1902. This grew out of classes organised by another notable philanthropist,

Tunbridge Wells Old Town Hall in Calverley Road, decorated for the Diamond Jubilee, 1897.

Dr George Abbott, at the Ear and Eye Hospital which he had also founded. Lutwidge, who helped to acquire the site, presented the new Institute with a stained glass window featuring allegorical representations of Science, Industry, Art and Commerce. Other products of the Victorian adult education movement were the Mechanics' Institute in Dudley Road, which held the town's original public library (adopted by the Council in 1921), and the Museum, another facility pioneered by George Abbott and adopted by the Council in 1918.

Monson Road Baths, laying of foundation stone, 1897

Technical Institute 1902, now Adult Education Centre.

George Abbott's Ear and Eye Hospital, opened in 1878 in Vale Road and making its final move to Mount Sion in 1900, was one of the two component institutions that came together to form a new town hospital in the 1930s. The other was the General Hospital, founded as a Dispensary in 1829 and moving to Grosvenor Road in 1842, where it underwent several enlargements. The new Kent and Sussex Hospital, opened on Mount Ephraim in 1934, was the largest building project hitherto undertaken in the town and a source of great pride to the local residents who had made it possible. At this period, prior to the advent of the welfare state, the local health service was entirely supported by subscriptions and donations. Fund-raising events included the Tunbridge Wells and District Football League's Charity Cup competition and the annual Hospital Sunday Carnival Parade organised by the Friendly Societies.

Prior to the opening of the Assembly Hall in 1939, venues for theatrical performances had been provided by private initiative. Sarah Baker's old theatre on the Lower Walk of the Pantiles had closed in 1843, to be succeeded by multi-purpose buildings like the Great Hall (1870-2) and the Pump Room (1877-8) which also hosted concerts, lectures and social events. Pelton's Guide in the 1870s speaks of 'four commodious and handsome public halls (including the Sussex Assembly Rooms and the Corn Exchange) where concerts of classical, popular and vocal music are given by speculators from London, by professional and amateur societies, and by private musicians, as well as under the auspices of local institutions and enterprising tradesmen of the town.'

By the 1890s, however, these were widely regarded as inadequate, and there was talk of building a new purpose-made theatre to celebrate Victoria's Diamond Jubilee. Delays resulted in a flamboyant Edwardian structure, opened in 1902 and known as the Opera House. According to contemporary witness Charles Strange, it was given this name because 'many of the good people of Tunbridge Wells looked askance at any sort of theatrical performance.'

Early plans for the building featured a gas-fired perpetual flame on the central dome. Pelton's Guide described it as 'a very elegant theatre and

The Opera House, Tunbridge Wells, c.1902.

decorated and fitted with great taste and in quite the modern up-to-date style' with its 1100 seats upholstered in crimson plush. The Opera House was converted into a cinema in 1931, but continued to be used for some stage productions. (It subsequently became a Bingo Hall in the 1970's, before being preserved and converted in the 1990's into a very imaginative Wetherspoon pub, retaining its Proscenium Arch, Boxes, Circle and Upper Circle.) As a cinema, it competed with the pre-existing Kosmos in Calverley Road and soon with the large modern Ritz, opened on the corner of Church Road and Mount Pleasant in 1934.

Following the successful inauguration of the town's publicly owned electricity system, the Improvement Association and the Tradesmen's Association urged the Council to pursue its progressive policy by setting up what would be the first municipal telephone system in England.

Although telephone services were already available in Tunbridge Wells, there was widespread dissatisfaction with the performance of the private National Telephone Company. Inspired by the success of a similar undertaking in Guernsey, launched in 1898, the Council agreed. The new system was inaugurated by Frank Green, Lord Mayor of London, at a ceremony at the Great Hall on 27 July 1901. The approaches to the Great Hall were decorated, and when the Lord Mayor arrived by train the local police and fire brigades provided a guard of honour. In his speech, Frank Green characterised the event as being of

The Municipal Switchboard in 1901.

national importance, declaring that 'he did not entertain for one moment the slightest doubt that what they had done in Tunbridge Wells would be copied – and speedily copied – by all other municipalities.' As a demonstration of the new technology, the Lord Mayor had a phone conversation with the Lord Provost of Glasgow, a city which was also pioneering a municipal system.

The subsequent controversy over whether the new telephone system represented value for money for the ratepayers brought the Council's progressive policy to an abrupt halt. In 1902 Colonel Trevenen Holland founded the Ratepayers' League to campaign against 'municipal trading', and this pressure group lobbied hard to sell off the system to the National Company.

The two local newspapers, the progressive *Advertiser* and its opponent *The Courier*, provided a public forum for the debate, featuring angry letters from both sides and editorial text attacking each other as well as the opposing party. Following an election in which candidates supported by the Ratepayers' League won a notable victory, the Council voted in November 1902 to allow the National Telephone Company to take over the municipal system.

Having won their first battle, the Ratepayers' League then embarked upon a campaign to sell off the local electricity system to private enterprise, with the local press once again providing a mouthpiece for both sides. In this case, however, the progressives were better organised, and moreover the electricity undertaking was well-established rather than a recent innovation.

Ultimately the campaign failed, because a majority of councillors and residents agreed that municipal electricity represented value for money. There were fears too that if the electricity undertaking was sold, the waterworks, sewerage farms and other public assets might follow.

In 1904, the Council set up an Improvement Committee 'to consider what can be done to bring Tunbridge Wells to the front again, and to bring it abreast with other watering places. There was talk of 'spending a large sum of money in equipping an installation of baths, which shall be amongst the most perfect and the most up-to-date in Europe, along with a Kursaal or Winter Garden, where concerts of a high-class description will be provided, and where there shall be an orchestra and other attractions for visitors.'

However, following the rise of the Ratepayers' League, the political climate was unfavourable to such ambitious proposals. As a cynical editorial in the *Advertiser* put it at the end of the year, 'Nothing could have exceeded the enthusiasm which that big idea created, but how tamely it has fizzled out to be sure.' Nonetheless, efforts were made to market the town's existing attractions more effectively, and a Borough Advertising Association was launched in 1908.

It was the Advertising Association which first suggested that an effective way of raising the town's national prestige would be to seek permission to use the prefix Royal, in recognition of the town's long association with royalty since the early days of its fame as a spa. The Council was keen to adopt this idea and voted to send a formal petition to Edward VII. The original proposal was that the town should be renamed *Royal Kentish Spa*, but the king preferred *Royal Tunbridge Wells*, and this was the name formally granted on 8 April 1909. *The Courier's* enthusiastic report concluded by saying: 'We trust that the prosperity and importance of Tunbridge Wells as the Royal Kentish Health Resort will be enhanced by the honour which has been done it.'

The First World War, in contrast to the Second, brought little or no physical damage to the town. A single Zeppelin dropped three bombs in Calverley Park, but these resulted in no more than broken windows. Nonetheless, the effect of the loss of 776 lives on active service should not be underestimated.

Contemporary witness Charles Strange's brief but vivid evocation of wartime Tunbridge Wells speaks of this period as 'a four-years' nightmare'. 'Soldiers' he says 'were collected here from all parts of England to be drafted across to France; our local volunteers – Territorials and Yeomanry – were mobilised and sent to all sections of the battle front; our empty houses became billets; imitation enemies were strung on lines on the Common and in Calverley Park for the recruits to stab with their bayonets; the churches opened canteens; the streets were darkened at night and church services in the evenings were given up; businesses were closed; professional men found themselves with nothing to do.' As the fighting progressed, many wounded were brought to local hospitals, and some 150 Belgian refugees were housed and cared for.

The inter-World War period of 1919-1939 saw a continuation of the battle between the progressives and their opponents.

Development of the town's open spaces continued with the purchase in 1921 of what we know today as Calverley Grounds, following a public enquiry in which pressure groups on both sides put forward their arguments. Much of the work on landscaping the new park was carried out by unemployed labourers paid from the Mayor's Unemployment Fund.

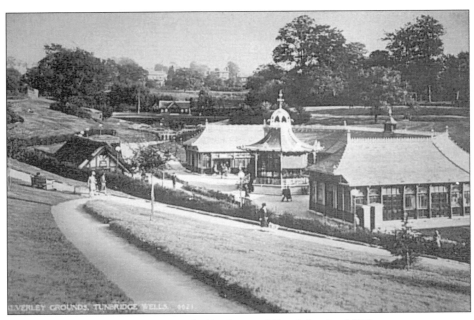

Calverley Grounds, Pavilion and Bandstand, c.1927.

In the autumn of 1922, the Council organised a competition to design an ambitious concert pavilion with an integral bandstand on one side, which would be large enough to seat two thousand people. Although there were forty entries in the competition, and a winner was selected, there was strong opposition led by the Ratepayers' League. The Council decided not to proceed but to look for a less expensive option. As an interim measure, a bandstand adorned with ornamental ironwork was erected in 1924, and work on a matching pavilion to provide covered accommodation for concert audiences began in the following year. The new pavilion was opened in April 1926.

The last major battle was over plans for a new Civic Centre complex, which would not only replace the long outdated Town Hall in Calverley Road, but also provide a new Police Station, Library, Museum and Assembly Hall. Part of the site, occupied by Decimus Burton's Calverley Parade, had been purchased as long ago as 1895, during Sir David Salomons' mayoralty.

In 1930 the Council voted to proceed with this long anticipated project, and demolition work to clear the site began in the following year. However, two months before the local elections of November 1931, the newly formed Burgesses' Emergency Association (closely linked with the Ratepayers' League) announced that they would be putting up their own candidates to oppose those who had voted for the proposed scheme.

Public interest in the election fight was intense. According to the *Advertiser*, the debate 'has lit up the town, and the war is being waged on both sides with what may be termed relentless ferocity.' *The Daily Mirror* reported, even more colourfully, that 'the campaign is so intensive that everyone, from rheumatic warriors in bath-chairs to boy warriors on bicycles, seems to be actively engaged.' Amid bitter accusations of lies and misinformation, six councillors seeking re-election were defeated by the Emergency Association's candidates.

Over the next few years, supporters of the Civic Centre scheme regrouped, and the Chamber of Trade led a fresh campaign to restart the project. Public opinion turned in favour of development, opposition on the Council dwindled, and in 1934 the Council announced an architectural competition to produce designs for the new complex. Architects Percy Thomas and Ernest Prestwich won the competition, and in July 1936 the Council voted to approve their scheme, subject to government approval for a loan. At the subsequent public enquiry in February 1937, no opposition was offered and the proceedings were completed in a little over two hours.

The way was now clear for building to begin. At the opening of the first completed section, the Assembly Hall, in May 1939, the Mayor, Charles Westbrook, declared that 'today's proceedings mark a definite step forward and a progressive policy.' He hoped people would now 'realise that we are not a dead borough, but really alive.'

The new Civic Centre complex
(Town Hall, Assembly Hall, Magistrates' Court, Library and Museum and Art Gallery.)

CHAPTER 12

THE SECOND WORLD WAR AND ITS AFTERMATH:
1939 – 1953

by Ann Bates

Tunbridge Wells in the Second World War was in a very different position from the one it had held in the First World War.

It found itself in the front-line of defence against the very serious risk of a German invasion. Tunbridge Wells was in a Forward Defence Area and was the Headquarters of XII Corps, charged with the defence of Kent and Sussex against invasion. It was also a Regional Centre of Government, as set up by the British Government. Early on, the town received hundreds of child evacuees from London (while getting them out of London is understandable, it is puzzling that so many were sent towards the enemy, rather than away from him). Slightly later, in mid-1940, it witnessed the Battle of Britain being fought in the skies above and it was surrounded throughout the War by RAF airfields (nearly all fighter airfields) which were in a constant state of alert. Later in 1944, Tunbridge Wells witnessed the largely-successful interception by the RAF of many of the German V-1 flying bombs – sadly the RAF were never able to catch up with the V-2 rocket. It was also host to many of the Allied troops making preparations for D-Day in June 1944. So Tunbridge Wells was really in the thick of it, as far as the Second World was concerned.

Yet it escaped remarkably lightly, with little loss of life or damage. It also suffered less in another respect – only 166 names were subsequently added to the 776 already on its First World War Memorial.

In April 1939, the Council formed an Emergency Committee of four, two Aldermen and two Councillors, to run the town on a day-to-day basis, in the event of war. It was chaired by the Mayor, Alderman C. E. Westbrook, who was to remain Mayor throughout the duration of the war, resigning in 1945. The first meeting was held on 1 September 1939 and initially met every morning. Later, meetings became less frequent, the last being on 24 October 1945.

Before war was declared on 3 September 1939, the Borough Council had been making preparations for Civil Defence. A Home Office Circular of 9th. July 1935 recommended Local Authorities to set up Air Raid Precaution (A.R.P.) committees and prepare plans to deal with the effects

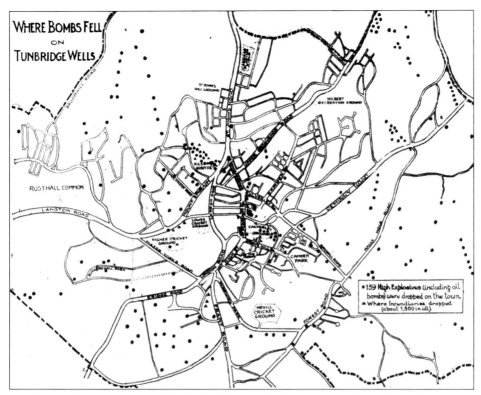

WHERE BOMBS FELL
ON
TUNBRIDGE WELLS

• 159 **High Explosives** (including oil bombs) were dropped on the town.
▲ Where Incendiaries dropped (about 1,500 in all).

Map indicating where the bombs fell, fortunately, largely outside residential areas.

of air raids. *The Courier* reported that the Borough Surveyor had been active to make things as safe as possible: 'The first steps taken at the commencement of the present crisis on 23 August 1939 were to provide facilities for the movement of traffic under blackout conditions'. This later led to kerbs, trees and other obstructions including mud guards on cars being painted in matt white. (Later in January 1941, further lighting regulations on vehicles were published.)

On 8 September 1939, *The Courier* printed a full page announcement giving advice and instructions on the course of actions to be taken during the War. Throughout the first months of the war, *The Courier* continued to publish announcements advising the public on such things as evacuation procedures, registration for food rationing, air raid warnings, emergency bus and train time tables, restricted postal services, fire services and shop hours. By the beginning of December 1939, the first reports of local servicemen being killed and wounded appeared. Throughout all the emergency preparations and reports of the war, the lead up to Christmas carried on almost as usual, with local shops advertising their wares.

A major subject for announcement was the evacuation of schoolchildren from London. The main reception point for children evacuees arriving from London, mainly at the West Station, was The Pump Room, near The Pantiles, where they were given a medical examination before going to other dispersal sites. The number of evacuees allotted for Tunbridge Wells was 5,598 but this number was not reached; some never arrived, and many had returned home after a short time. By January 1940, there were only 855 school children in the Borough from London.

Amongst the schools to be evacuated to Tunbridge Wells were Blackheath High School for Girls, who joined up with the Tunbridge Wells High School for Girls (which had been in financial difficulties before the war, and finally closed in 1945); Colfe's Boys' School from Lewisham who joined Skinners; and The Blue Coat School who were at Culverden House. Guy's Hospital Medical School was evacuated and situated at Sherwood in Pembury Road, with the students being housed at Hurstmead, and two other houses in Sandrock Road. Lectures were held in the basement of the newly built Baptist Tabernacle in Upper Grosvenor Road, and qualified Doctors and Nurses from the School joined Pembury Hospital.

[Later, in July 1944, evacuation was resumed during the V1 and V2 bombardments, with children from Tunbridge Wells being evacuated to the West Country. Somewhat paradoxically and at the same time, Tunbridge Wells became again a reception area for schoolchildren from London. The evacuees did not return to London until May 1945.]

Food rationing (which had been planned since 1936, in case of war) began on 8 January 1940 with sugar, butter and bacon as the first items, followed by meat in March, and tea, margarine, cooking fats and many other items in July.

In January 1940, the Emergency Committee reported that the revenue and capital expenditure on the ARP for nine months to 31 December 1939 had been £38,127, much of which had been covered by Government grants, but it still left £6,229 to be found by the Council. For the people of Tunbridge Wells life seemed to be relatively normal. After Christmas, the Winter Sales (in those days, Sales were only twice a year) commenced as usual. Towards the end of January and the beginning of February 1940, there were heavy snowfalls in the area disrupting traffic. There were to be heavy snowfalls in the following winters of 1941 and 1942, with severe frosts.

Bredbury

Tunbridge Wells became a Regional Centre of Government. As Hitler's forces advanced through France, hurried defence preparations were made. Tunbridge Wells was located between what was called the forward 'stop line' and the GHQ line. At 'Bredbury' on Mount Ephraim, the Regional HQ of No 12 [South Eastern] Civil Defence Region was established. This department co-ordinated the many Civil Defence organisations in the area throughout the war, and would have been of prime importance in the event of an invasion. Defences planned for Tunbridge Wells included concrete lined trenches in the Calverley Grounds, trenches elsewhere in the town, and tank obstructions, known as Dragon's Teeth, located at strategic road junctions.

In March 1940, the then Prime Minister, Neville Chamberlain, together with the Home Secretary, Sir John Anderson [of Anderson Shelter fame], paid a visit to Bredbury, and were greeted by Sir Auckland Geddes [later Lord Geddes 1879 – 1954], the Regional Controller and his deputy Lord Knollys [1895 – 1966] and other officials. Later in the day, Sir John Anderson met the Mayor and Town Clerk Mr John Whitehead, at the Borough Control Room, and saw the new Police Station and Police Court. In July 1941 Sir Auckland Geddes was taken ill, and was replaced by Lord Monsell [1881 – 1969], who remained as Regional Controller until he retired in April 1945. Another notable visitor to Bredbury was HRH the Duke of Kent in May 1941, and there were many other Royal and Ministerial visitors through out the war.

King George VI visiting Tunbridge Wells, June 1941. Montgomery on right of picture.

XII Corps, which consisted of 2 Divisions (in total some 20-25,000 soldiers), each with 3 Infantry Brigades, each with 4 Infantry Battalions, and with supporting Cavalry (i.e. Armoured) and Artillery regiments, had been designated as the defenders of the Kent and Sussex coastline against invasion; and sensibly Tunbridge Wells which in location straddled both Kent and Sussex, was chosen as the Corps

Montgomery at El Alamein.

HQ. The Corps was commanded by a Lieutenant-General. It had had at least two of these, before it received in April 1941 its most famous General Officer Commanding (G.O.C.) – a certain Lieut. General Bernard Montgomery, later to be better known as Field-Marshal Viscount Montgomery of Alamein. His H.Q and the Officers' Mess were at No. 10, Broadwater Down, and it was here on 13 June 1941 that King George VI paid a visit. Later in the afternoon, the King visited the Mechanised Transport Corps unit in Birling Road, which was made up of women drivers. No. 69, Warwick Park had been requisitioned as the living quarters for the G.O.C. and Montgomery was to live there from April to November 1941, before being promoted to command for the next eight months the South Eastern Army, defending the whole of the Southern coast. He was promoted yet again in August 1942 to command the Eight Army in North Africa, where he won an overwhelming victory over Rommel's forces at El Alamein in October-November 1942.

There was a secret War project taking place in Broadwater Down, of which Montgomery later denied any knowledge and it is highly

.A flooded 'Wilderness' tunnel in 1996.

probable that he was totally unaware of it. 'The Wilderness', on land in Hargate Forest which had been requisitioned at the start of the war from the Abergavenny Eridge Estate, was a series of underground tunnels which were planned to be used as a communications centre. The tunnels were excavated by 20 men of the 172 Tunnelling Company of the R.E. who were billeted at Mount Edgcombe. They started in 1940 and finished the following year. It is thought that the centre was never used, and the land was returned to the Eridge Estate in 1945. The entrances to the tunnels can still be seen, and in 1996 the site was visited and surveyed by the 'Subterranea Britannica' Society *(www.subterranea britannica.com)*.

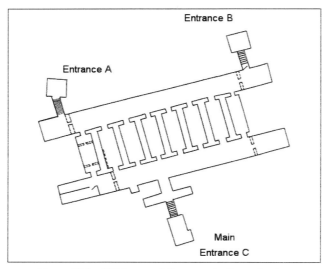

Plan of "The Wilderness" Communications Centre.

Another little-known form of defence were the XII Corps Observation Units or Auxiliary Units, set up to fight a guerilla war after invasion, which had secret hideouts [called Deneholes] for use in the event of invasion. There were many throughout Kent. Whether there were any in the Tunbridge Wells area is still not known. Men in these units had to sign the Official Secrets Act, and although they were officially part of the Home Guard, their duties were unknown to their colleagues.

In early May 1940 the first local man to win a medal for bravery, Pilot Officer P. Smith R.A.F. of Culverden Down, was awarded the Distinguished Flying Cross (DFC). By the end of the month, the evacuation of Dunkirk was under way and *The Courier* gave weekly reports of local men who had been rescued, together with those killed, wounded, missing and gaining gallantry awards. It was decided to post lists of civilian casualties at the Police Station.

In June 1940, the Removal of Direction Signs Order [1940] was passed. All road and direction signposts were removed throughout the country; and town maps and names on Council vehicles were also removed. This was meant to deprive invading forces of any indication of where they were, but since there was never to be an invasion, it probably confused everybody, except locals, much more.

Bomb crater in Calverley Grounds.

Reports of air attacks appeared in *The Courier*, though the locality was never given, due to censorship rules. Amongst the first in the town was a bomb which dropped in the Calverley Grounds causing a large crater in a flower bed. Later in November 1940, an oil bomb was dropped and this destroyed The Pavilion.

Throughout the summer of 1940, the Battle of Britain was at its height and a number of incidents were reported in the Borough. Two were killed and two slightly injured on 11 September, but the worst occurred next day when at 5.10 pm, a lone German bomber probably on its way from (or maybe still on its way to) London released 22 bombs and 22 incendiaries in a path stretching from Connaught Way to Great Culverden Park to the Hospital to Grosvenor Road. Twelve were killed, two seriously injured and 14 slightly injured. The Kent and Sussex

Spitfire, named Royal Tunbridge Wells, bought by public subscription.

Hospital was damaged in this attack. In the same month, a 500 kg. D/A H.E. [Delayed Action High Explosive] bomb was dropped near the Hastings railway line behind Forest Road, and as a result the line was closed for 10 days. In the early years of the war, special ambulance and evacuation trains were kept in the extensive goods-yard at the West Station (now Sainsbury's), but later these were moved to Sevenoaks.

By the end of the summer of 1940, the heavy day-time raids were over, and the nightly raids on London began. It was possible to see the red glow in the night sky over London from Rusthall Common.

Advertisement in 'The Courier',
December 1940.

Various 'fund' weeks became a feature in the Town throughout the war.

The first started on 9 August 1940, when the Mayor launched a 'Spitfire Fund' to 'buy' a Spitfire for the RAF, and it had raised £5,031(equivalent to about £120,000 in 2005, but more than enough to 'buy' a Spitfire in those days) when it closed on 29 September.

The second was 'War Weapons Week', which was held between 13th. and 20th. December 1940. There was an opening ceremony and an exhibition which included a shot-down German aircraft on show in the new library building which was not yet in use (it was not opened until after the war). £510,224 (about £13 million at 2005 values) was raised in just one week, an enormous amount for just one town.

Others weeks included:
* ❖ Warship Week: 28th. February to 7th. March 1942: when it was hoped that £450,000 or more would be raised for a destroyer. This was successfully achieved and as a result, H.M.S. Brilliant which had already been commissioned, was 'adopted' by Tunbridge Wells. [£17 – 4 – 0d per head [equivalent to £430 at 2005 values] was given in Tunbridge Wells, the highest in Kent];

Shot down Messerschmidt 109 being taken into the Library building for display in War Weapons Week, 1940.

❖ 'Wings for Victory' Week in May 1943 when on average, £12 – 5 – 0d per head [£310 at 2005 values] was raised.

❖ In January 1943 there was a book drive for 100,000 books. These were required to replace books lost in bombed libraries, and for servicemen.

❖ 'Salute the Soldier' Week was held in June 1944 with a full programme of events aimed to raise £450,000; and other funds included A Prisoner of War Fund, and a Ship Adoption Society.

Support organizations were also set up. The Tunbridge Wells War Comforts Association sent 48,000 cigarettes to servicemen in the forces. The Tunbridge Wells Knitting Society over the years produced thousands of garments for the services and bombed-out families, providing over 35,000 garments by 1944.

There was also concern about pedestrians on the roads in the blackout. In September 1939, Kent County Council reported that there had been a 73% increase in traffic accidents compared to 1938, one of those involved being 'Sir Auckland Geddes (the Regional Controller of Civil Defence) run down by a lady cyclist, while inspecting ARP measures in Hastings'. Orders were also placed with local builders to build twenty-two Air Raid Warden posts.

Children in St. Mark's Primary School Air Raid Shelter.

In September 1940, air-raid shelters for the public were provided in the town, one of which was under the newly built Civic Centre. The caves under 'St. Helena' opposite Dudley Road, were opened but later were closed because of the damp. St. Mark's Parish Hall was amongst the first of the First-Aid Posts and there was a decontamination station at The Kent and Sussex Hospital. In November 1940, the Borough Council considered a scheme to provide more accommodation for 1000 bunks in Air Raid Shelters.

Other restrictions included Kite Flying and the ringing of Church bells and in September 1940 by order of the S.E. Regional Commissioner, theatres, cinemas, public houses, and restaurants were to close at 10pm. In homes, windows were taped to prevent flying glass. It was also recommended that water buckets, sand buckets and stirrup pumps should be on hand to cope with incendiary bombs.

Men not already in the Services, between 17 – 65 years of age were required to register at the Police Station as Local Defence Volunteers. In two days, 500 had 'signed on' in Tunbridge Wells. The following year [1941], a Civil Defence Duties Compulsory Enrolment Order was issued and men between 18-60 were obliged to register by 3 May. This was followed in January 1942 by the direction into essential employment of girls aged 21 and over. About 400 registered in Tunbridge Wells. They had the choice of ATS [Auxiliary Territorial Service] attached to the Army, WAAF [Women's Auxiliary Air Force], WRNS [Women's Royal Naval

Service], the Land Army, Civil Defence or industry. Even before this, women had joined up or taken over many jobs, including delivering milk and letters, releasing men for active service.

Salvage drives were part of town life. In April 1941 at the instigation of the 'dynamic' Lord Beaverbrook, the Minister for Aircraft Production, iron railings were forcibly collected throughout the country. Exemption was given to historic examples and those where removal would cause danger to the public. In Tunbridge Wells, the Emergency Committee dealt with many appeals against removal, and in the minutes, addresses are listed. Those removed included the Victorian drinking fountain in Grosvenor Recreation Ground and the remains of the Bandstand in Calverley Grounds. Others to disappear were the railings from Holy Trinity Church and King Charles the Martyr, and many were removed from houses throughout the town. This changed the appearance of the town forever. Even today it is possible to see where the railings were roughly cut off, much to the displeasure of many residents. Applications could be made to the Ministry of Supply via the Town Clerk for compensation which was 25/- [£1-25p] per ton. Not only iron railings were salvaged, but metal of all kinds, including tin cans and saucepans, were collected. The irony is that much of the metal collected was

'Steam-rollering' tins, saucepans, and other metal collected in Tunbridge Wells, 1941.

unsuitable for reprocessing, but it certainly helped people to think that they were making a sacrifice for the War Effort.

Old Tunbridge Wells Rate Books 1889-1913 going for salvage – a matter of great regret for local historians.

In 1942, Mr. E. B. Weekes (Chairman of Weekes department store, now Hoopers since 1986) as Chairman of the Salvage Committee started a waste paper drive and announced that children would be admitted free to a film show at the Opera House if they arrived with not less than 2lbs of paper. In the event, the average per child was 6lbs and by July, 4 tons 3 cwt of paper had been collected.

Boy Scouts collecting salvage – some 30 tons of paper.

Many buildings in the area were requisitioned to become auxiliary hospitals, hostels and other establishments including 25, Frant Road, previously St. Clair Ladies Private School; and The Manor House [Manor Grange], Hurstwood Lane, which was opened as an auxiliary Hospital. In August 1944, it was damaged by a Flying Bomb, and by October it was empty. Ferndale Point [No.2 Ferndale] was requisitioned as an evacuee hostel in November 1942, but an outbreak of Scabies was reported and a few months later the Ministry of Health Welfare Officer recommended that Ferndale Point should be closed, which it was in May 1943. In January 1943, No. 17, Landsdowne Road was inspected and the Ministry of Health approved it for the establishment of a war-time nursery. The Town Clerk was instructed to requisition the house, remove the furniture and make necessary alterations and repairs, and engage staff. It remained a nursery until closed by the KCC in December 1949, a move deplored by the Borough Council.

In Broadwater Down, the Army requisitioned No. 2 as an Officer' billet, No. 10 as the Army HQ and Officers' Mess, and No. 13 as an army billet. Dunorlan House was also requisitioned in 1943. Mr Carteret Collins, the last owner of Dunorlan had died in February 1941 and the estate had been sold to the Borough Council. It was initially occupied by troops who reputedly used the cornices, gables, statues and ornaments for target practice. Subsequently and somewhat ironically, it became the HQ of the War Damage Commission. It was not returned to the Council until 1958, but as early as June 1950, the Parks Committee had discussed the possibility that it should be the venue for public entertainment.

Dunorlan Park in the 1870s.

Before the War, Rusthall Beacon, Tea Garden Lane (now The Beacon Restaurant) had housed 60 Basque refugee children from the Spanish Civil War. They were followed later by a group of Jewish children. Other premises earmarked by the Ministry of Health were The Wellington Hotel and Hamilton House, although these were not used. Suggestions made by the Emergency Committee and decisions taken by them included in 1942, sites for a reserve hospital, a Field Dressing Station on The Common, emergency feeding stations, special rest centres for use under invasion conditions, and estimates and approval of expenditure on domestic air raid shelters. The Minutes of the Emergency Committee also list applications for the issue of Anderson (outdoor corrugated-iron) and Morrison (indoor steel-plate-and-grill) air-raid shelters, and the number of these which were distributed to residents.

As the war years dragged on, rationing and restrictions became more stringent and long queues at shops and bus stops were a normal sight in the Town. Even tea shops were not immune. In 1941, fines were imposed on a butcher for selling 3lbs 10ozs of pork contrary to Rationing Orders, and on a woman for throwing away 2lbs of cheese and bread.

Advertisements appeared asking people to grow more food and part of the Culverden Golf Course was ploughed up to grow potatoes. A National Food Effort was announced asking households to save kitchen waste to feed pigs and poultry. With regular local collections been made, housewives saved everything. Shops were unable to obtain paper bags and string, so customers took their own. Unlike today, most goods were not then prepacked.

Early in 1943, concern was shown over the use of water, and it was thought that the supply would have to be limited. *The Courier* continued to publish announcements giving guidance on the saving of fuel, electricity, and food facts. Holiday travel was also discouraged. In the early part of the war, petrol rationing had limited the use of cars to 200 miles per month. Later after March 1942, petrol for private use was withdrawn completely.

Bus queue on Mount Pleasant by Lonsdale Gardens.

Bus services were restricted, with no Sunday services before 1 pm, and on weekdays there was a 9 pm curfew. It was said that the new restrictions would make little material change as similar ones were already in force. It should be remembered that there had been no street lighting since the beginning of the war. There were no shop window lights; and permission for these was not restored until April 1949.

The Emergency Committee reported to the Council that the cost of Civil Defence in the Borough in 1943-4 had amounted to £68,043, of which £44,425 had been paid by the Government and with grants and other income estimated at £16,270, this left £7,348 to be provided by the Council. This was equivalent to 4d [1½p.] in the £ on the local rates.

In April there had been wholesale theft of rationed goods from a Southern Railway Goods Yard. The name of the Goods Yard was not mentioned for censorship reasons, but the men named lived in the High Brooms area. Concern was expressed that this would lead to a Black Market, which was somewhat naive since one had existed, depending on who and what you knew,

Queueing for Ration Books in Tunbridge Wells.

since the early days of the war.

Though it was still two years before the War would end, discussions were already being held, on how life would/should be in peacetime. These included debating the Beveridge Report which would be a blueprint for the future Welfare State; council housing schemes; and the Tunbridge Wells Chamber of Trade discussed 'The Post War Development of Tunbridge Wells' at their annual meeting.

In November 1942, the Civic Association (the forerunner of the Royal Tunbridge Wells Civic Society) had been invited by the Town Council to prepare proposals for the post-war development of the Town. In a report of some 80 pages published in 1943, and edited by Helen Spalding, were included sketches and plans of many major projects including a repertory theatre, Winter Garden, the rebuilding and refurbishment of The Pantiles, (including the area which was rebuilt in the 1980's), the High Street, and even then, they were not happy with the Cinema site.

Housing including the demolition and rebuilding of the whole of the St. Peters area, schools, playing fields and sport facilities, and car parks were also covered in the Report. The flow of traffic was also discussed and it was suggested that many of the major roads in the Town should be widened, particularly in the shopping areas, and a by-pass of the Town to the South West, should be made to relieve the overcrowding on the A26 (even in 1943!). A municipal airport was also considered, with helicopters being the main choice of aircraft!

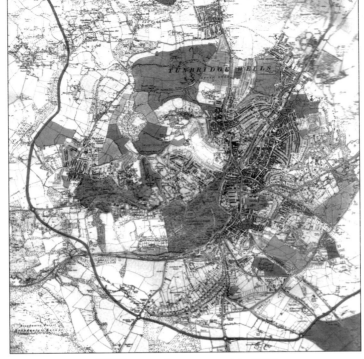

A26 Bypass plan, proposed in 1943.

In August 1943, a ban restricting admittance without written authority was re-imposed on a large area of S.E. England, with residents been issued with passes. Although not stated at the time, this security was clearly to do with preparations for D-Day.

1944 began, with night air-raids causing casualties and damage. These continued to be reported in *The Courier* and pictures appeared regularly but no names or addresses were given, but it can be assumed that they must have been in the local area.

Again, concern was shown on the use of water, and there were fears that supplies would have to be limited. As in previous years, announcements were published advising the public on electricity, food, saving fuel and the allowances of coal and coke per household, and the distribution of new ration books. There was also reported to be 'a growing Rat menace' in the Town. In March, the Council Rates were announce for the coming year, this was to be 11 shillings and 5 pence [57p] in the £, and it was estimated that the cost of Civil Defence was equal to 4d. (1½ p.) The public were euphemistically 'asked' not to travel during the Easter and Whitsun holidays; and announcements were published to this effect.

As D-Day [6 June 1944] approached, there was much military activity in the area. This included an evacuation hospital established in Langton Green by the Americans. It seems strange that editions of *The Courier* published later in the month made no mention of the D-Day landings, although reports of local men involved, started to appear. The first Flying Bomb [V1] was recorded on 30th June 1944. These would continue together with the V2 rockets until the end of March 1945, when the last V2 fell.

Because air raid shelters were being used by vagrants and as rubbish tips, the Emergency Committee decided that these should be closed except during raids, and the Town Clerk was asked to draw up rules and regulations for the use of shelters. Earlier they had received a report that the shelter in Albion Road was being used for unspecified 'immoral purposes'.

One outstanding award for gallantry at this time was the Victoria Cross awarded to Capt. L. E. Queripel of the 10th Battalion, Parachute Regiment and The Royal Sussex Regiment, who was killed at Arnhem in September 1944. He is buried at Oosterbeek Cemetery and is commemorated in the Book of Remembrance in the Town Hall. His parents lived for many of years at 52, Warwick Park.

Though the Allies were advancing into Europe, damage caused by Flying Bombs and V2 rockets was still being reported. News was

VE Day Service in Calverley Grounds.

coming through of local men, who had been prisoners of war in Germany, being released. The many groups involved in Civil Defence were being stood down, and by the middle of May, VE (Victory in Europe) Day, numerous parades and celebrations were held in various parts of the Town. These included Church services, street parties, parades and bonfires on the Common. When VJ (Victory over Japan) Day was declared in August, again there were many parties and parades. Gradually the men who had been prisoners of war in the Far East also returned. And 166 names of local men who had been killed were to be added to the First World War Memorial.

At the end of the War, it was reported by the Kent County Council Civil Defence Department that in Tunbridge Wells during the War, there had been:

❖ 15 killed, 31 seriously injured and 36 slightly injured.
❖ 13 properties destroyed
❖ 113 severely damaged
❖ 738 houses had been damaged,
❖ and 5,488 slightly damaged (mainly broken windows).

Some 186 H.E. (high-explosive) bombs, and approximately 660 incendiary bombs (most in the summer and autumn of 1940) and 6 flying bombs had fallen on the Town; and 5 enemy aircraft had crashed in the area. Some of their crews had parachuted to safety and had been taken prisoner.

There is no doubt that for a town so close to the front-line, Tunbridge Wells had got off lightly.

Home Guard 'Stand-down' Parade on 26th June 1945.

160

In November 1945, the first Borough Elections since 1938 took place. The Mayor, Alderman Charles Westbrook O.B.E. J.P., retired after being in office for eight years and understandably did not seek re-election. A General Election had taken place on July 5th 1945, when a Labour government had been returned. But Tunbridge Wells (or more precisely the Tonbridge constituency, of which Tunbridge Wells was then part) remained staunchly Conservative, and Gerald Williams was returned as the local M.P.

Alderman Charles Westbrook.

Also in November 1945, a National Savings Thanksgiving week was held. It was the fifth such week held since 1940, and raised £645,000 (equivalent to £14 million at 2005 values). It was announced that the total war savings raised in Tunbridge Wells to the end of 1944 amounted to £8,207,510 or £230 per head (or approximately £175 million, or £5,000 per head, at 2005 values)

So the war years ended, but it was not the end of shortages and rationing for the people of Tunbridge Wells. In fact, in many ways, things became much worse and the whole country faced ten years of real economic austerity, although on a decreasing scale. Food rationing, which had been in force since 1940, became more stringent. For example, bread which had never been rationed during the War

Captain Edward Westbrook Tunbridge Wells Fire Chief and father of Ald. Charles Westbrook.

was rationed for the first time in July 1946 and remained rationed for the next two years. Food rationing was not finally abolished until July 1954, with meat being one of the last to be de-rationed. Even so, early in 1946, buffet cars were reinstated on the trains to Hastings, the first time since 1941; the Emmanuel Canteen run by the Emmanuel Church on Mount Ephraim closed after six years of service to the Forces, and it was estimated that between 600,000 – 700,000 men had been served during that time; and the Tunbridge Wells Comfort Association was closed.

The Divisional Food Office in Bishops Down was visited by Dr. Edith Summerskill M.P., the Under-Secretary of the Ministry of Food in May. In July 1946, bread rationing was introduced, much to the concern of bakers and housewives. There was even a suggestion that greengrocery

"Dragon's Teeth" being removed outside the Post Office in late 1945.

should be rationed. The Ministry of Food continued to give guidance through its advertisements – one of which was five ways on how to use stale bread. Recruiting advertisements for the Land Army appeared for women between the ages of 17 – 40 years. They were required to enlist for 2 years service, and the rate of pay was 50/- shillings [£2 50p, or £55 at 2005 values] for a 48 hour week, plus overtime.

The Chamber of Trade called for unity in post-war planning, and there was a call for a Civic Week. The Council was discussing the building of houses on new housing estates. Amongst these were Powdermill Lane and Eridge Road [Ramslye] Estates. German and Italian prisoners-of-war worked on both these estates. Mr Aneurin Bevan, the Health Minister attended a conference at the Assembly Hall on Housing. Another subject discussed was the impending introduction of the National Health Service, and the problem of the supply of electricity. Again January 1946 had been very cold, and there was a lack of school places. Discussions were held in September regarding a suitable war memorial, and it was suggested that a social centre, garden of remembrance and shrine should be built at Dunorlan, and a fund be started with a minimum target of £25,000. In April there had been a serious fire at Dunorlan.

As in the war years, special weeks were held. A new target for National Savings was set amounting to £700,000 in twelve months (equivalent to £14 million today), while in the previous five years, £10 million had been saved (£200 million). Road Safety Week, and a Welcome Home Fund was launched by the Council.

An RAF Mosquito fighter-bomber crashed near a school in Rusthall. Fortunately none of the children were injured although the pilot, a local man, was killed. But there was some good news – V-Day celebrations and Cricket Week were held in June, the Open Tennis Tournament in July, and in November, Bonfire Night and a Festival of Remembrance at the Assembly Hall. The Tunbridge Wells Bowls Tournament was revived, and local football was once again in the news. An exhibition entitled 'Britain Can Make It' opened in London, surprising given that so many restrictions were still in place.

But as the New Year of 1947 started, coal rationing was introduced during the coldest winter for fifty years, and on the night of 23 February, Tunbridge Wells recorded a temperature of -19°C. There were major gas and electricity cuts, and prison was threatened for anyone found wasting electricity. It was recommended to have only one bath a week to save fuel, and to ease electricity consumption, Double Summer Time, which had been first introduced during the War, was reintroduced in March 1947. There were newsprint restrictions, throughout this period. *The Courier* consisted of just 8 broadsheet pages, and schools were hit by the paper shortage. After the long hard winter when the cost of clearing the snow had amounted to nearly £10,000, gales and floods followed in March, ruining many crops. Vegetables became scarce. Later there was to be a long hot dry summer.

The Lighting Committee of the Borough Council were concerned with the introduction of the Electricity Bill which nationalized electrical supply, including the local electricity company which was owned by the Council. While the Council had over time made a capital investment of £956,220 in the company, it was thought that the Council would only receive £29,958 in compensation and this was thought to be very unfair. The Kent and Sussex Hospital was reported to be in financial difficulties owing to a drop in donations, with expenses possibly reaching £90,000. In October assets of £30,000 were sold by the Hospital. There was also a lack of nurses and three wards had to close.

In September a woman was jailed, the Police describing her as a perfect nuisance to German POW's at their camp at Somerhill. Other subjects of public interest were the opening of cinemas on Sundays. A public meeting was held at which a vote was taken when the majority were in favour. At the time, Tunbridge Wells boasted four cinemas. [The Ritz, The Opera House, the Kosmos in Calverley Road, and the Great Hall.]

Again the subject of a War Memorial was raised, a plan by The British Legion at an estimated cost of £70,000 was approved by the Council, but there was a general lack of public interest and the scheme never materialized. Two other schemes proposed at the time were a new ex-servicemen's club, and a plan by Cecil Burns for the improvement of the existing memorial, but neither was implemented.

One feature of the time was that many major conferences were held in Tunbridge Wells, one of which was the South Eastern Regional Conference. attended by Hugh Gaitskell, then the Fuel Minister, but later the leader of the Labour Party. Calls for domestic and industrial fuel economies were made.

With the co-operation of the British Restaurant, a 'Meals on Wheels' service was started by the W.V.S. and was the first of its kind in Kent, starting with two meals a week at a cost of 1/- [5p, or £1.05 at 2005 values.]

August 1947 saw the Prime Minister, Mr. Attlee, announcing an Austerity Plan and emergency powers to increase production and reduce home consumption. There were further cuts in imports causing reductions in the meat and butter rations. A butcher was fined for contravening food orders. Later in the year, another trader was fined £350 in connection with the sale of oatmeal, for over charging, over supplying and not keeping records. In June, there was a cull of grey squirrels and these were sold for human consumption.

There were power cuts of 3 hours each morning and 2 hours in the afternoon when electric heaters could not be used. Petrol for private cars was withdrawn. In August 1946, the allowance had been 270 miles per month. In June 1948, the ration was restored to 90 miles per month. The Regional Petroleum Office which controlled petrol rationing and was located in the Pump Room on the Pantiles and at 25 Frant Road, received applications from 120,000 people asking for petrol coupons in September 1947 and the staff at the Pump Room were overwhelmed. The Petroleum Office continued until June 1950 when it closed after 11 years, with 130 permanent and 120 temporary staff being made redundant. The future of the Pump Room then became very uncertain and it was finally demolished in 1964, to be replaced by the out-of-character Union Square.

Internationally, there was a great deal of tension, called The Cold War by the media, between the Western Allies and the USSR; and consequently Britain re-introduced conscription under the name of National Service, initially for 12 months, then extended to 18 months and finally to 2 years.

The Courier reported on how this affected local men and also on other local issues. The housing shortage throughout 1947 brought it own problems. It was estimated that accommodation was needed for 4,000 people in the Town. The New Council estate at Powdermill Lane had been delayed by the bad weather in the early part of the year and would not be completed until 1948. The plan for the Eridge Road Estate was submitted to the Ministry for approval. It was hoped to build 400 houses together with a school, community hall, public house and at least 8 shops. Council house tenants were unhappy with the rent levels being charged and threatened to strike, and adding to the housing problem, there was wanton damaged being caused on the new housing estates. Squatters in Great Bounds Camp had their electricity supply cut, and it was not until September 1950 that these huts were demolished.

At Christmas, Tunbridge Wells received food parcels from Wellington, New Zealand, and Tasmania, including 50 cases of jam and tinned fruit and 7 cwts. of rolled oats.

For the first time in many years, the winter of 1948 was comparatively mild. The spring was very dry, and by early June, the Council was appealing for people to save water, once again. But only two weeks later, there was a severe storm in the area with many houses being struck by lighting and with flooding in the lower parts of the town. Reports of this appeared juxtaposed to the 'save water' advertisements. In August, there was a heat-wave, followed by heavy rain. Later in the month, a 70 mile-per-hour gale struck the South East, and in December there was the worst fog for 40 years.

The prisoner-of-war camp at Somerhill was capable of holding 1,500 prisoners and many German and Italian prisoners-of-war were still being held as late as 1947-8. Because of the labour shortage, many worked on farms, and building sites. Some 15 were used on the Eridge Road housing estate, but were withdrawn in March 1948.

In July 1948, the Kent and Sussex Hospital became part of the National Health Service, with some regret by the local population. The Hospital books showed that the cash balance was £10,000, with investments amounting to £52,000 and the building and equipment being valued at over half a million pounds.

Also in the summer of 1948, the XIVth Olympic Games were held in London, mainly at Wembley Stadium. They were shown on television, which was then black-and-white and only one Channel – now BBC1- but TV ownership was very low with less than one million TV sets in the UK. So it is not surprising that the Games seem to have had very little effect on the every-day life of the Town.

Towards the end of the year, the Minister of Works opened the Civil Service Regional Centre at Hawkenbury, the building of which had begun in 1941. This was a bunker intended to be a Regional Centre of UK Government in case of war. It was joined in 1963 by an eight-storey office building, which was to dominate the Hawkenbury (and even Tunbridge Wells) skyline for the next 35 years, until it was demolished to everyone's relief in 1997-8. Beneath the bunker was reputedly eight floors of offices and accommodation which were intended to be the Regional Centre of Government.

Princess Margaret visiting St. Christophers' Nursing Training College, Tunbridge Wells, October 1948.

Fortunately, it never had to be used. It took about 12 weeks of pneumatic drills and minor explosions to demolish it; and it is thought that many of the underground rooms at the lowest level remain intact. The site is now occupied by the Land Registry and some of the land was sold off for private housing.

As the winter of 1948-9 approached, it was feared that there would be electricity shortages again, and bakers warned of a bread shortage.

1949 started with the Council seeking to expand the borough boundaries to include Southborough, Bidborough, Speldhurst, and Pembury under the Local Government Boundary Commission Act of 1945. This would have increased the population from 38,080 to 52,064. The plan was strongly opposed by all the Parishes involved. Later in the year, the Boundary Commission was suddenly wound up, and the plan was dropped.

In February, The High Brooms Brick Works accepted a Government order for 3 million hand-made facing bricks for the new power station to be built at Southwick, near Brighton.

The first tenants moved into houses on the Ramslye Estate. There had been only two tenders for contracts submitted by local builders for the 62 houses involved, and the Council discussed using direct labour instead.

The summer was hot and vegetables were in short supply, with the gravest water shortage in 20 years. Rainfall had been deficient every year since 1939, except 1948, and ways of saving water were announced, including the advised depth of bath water, although how this could be checked within the bounds of decorum, was anybody's guess. True to form, there were severe storms later in the year and many areas of the town were flooded.

First woman Mayor,
Miss Muriel Wells.

In May, the Town's first woman Mayor, Miss Muriel Wells, was elected. She had been the local representative of the W.V.S. during the war. Again the Town was a popular place for conferences. They included the S.E. Division of the Local Education Authorities Association, addressed by the Minister of Education. 2000 members attended The British Legion County rally.

In the Medical Officer's report for 1949, it was stated that the death rate in Tunbridge Wells was higher than average, with 350 females and 235 men dying, possibly reflecting the age of the population in the Town.

Another report showed that unemployment was gradually creeping up with 144 men and 73 women registered as unemployed, though there were 120 vacancies mainly in the building and domestic trades. It was also reported that 386 more nurses were needed in the area.

With the Cold War at its height and the threat of atomic warfare, plans for bringing Civil Defence up to date with an Atomic Warfare Syllabus was discussed and it was agreed that recruiting would start in the Autumn.

Early in December 1949, 1000 young firs, the property of the Marquess of Abergavenny, were stolen from Broadwater Forest, and the following January the raiders were sent to prison. Other concerns were that

Pembury Hospital was uneconomical, the traffic problem in shopping streets, and the Chamber of Trade was alarmed at the growth of 'no waiting' restrictions.

The Ministry of Health reported to the Council that the Town's water was unsatisfactory 'owing to its iron content and its aggressive nature' and throughout May, this topic continued to cause concern. The many public events were well attended. In June, a Fete held at Dunorlan attracted a crowd of 10,000; the following month, the Agricultural Show also attracted large crowds; and the Tennis Tournament held at the Nevill Ground was described as the best ever, though the spectators had a lucky escape when lightning struck during a thunderstorm. The weather was also in the news in April when there were heavy snowfalls in the area. This caused the station clock to stop and it was not restarted until September.

Other topics discussed during the year were the establishment of a school at Huntley's, a new Council Estate of 394 houses at the junction of Sandhurst and Pembury Roads, and the building of the Ramslye Estate which had been delayed by the lack of cement. In Tunbridge Wells, 247 persons were listed as unemployed with a shortage in the building trades reported.

Throughout 1950 there were many visits of Ministry officials, as many official regional offices were still in the area, and the Assembly Hall continued to be the venue for conferences. But the big international news of the Korean War, which started in June 1950, seems to have had little impact on Tunbridge Wells.

Even six years after the war had ended, references were being made to a need for a reduction in the meat ration. There was still a fuel shortage and there was a warning advertisement in *The Courier* to this effect. 'The Festival of Britain' was opened in May 1951 on London South Bank, introducing new ideas in all areas of life. Tunbridge Wells Shopping Week was held in June, coinciding with the first Carnival for 14 years. The Tunbridge Wells and Southern Counties Agricultural Show was resumed for the first time since the war and was held on the permanent show ground site in Eridge Road [now the Showfields Estate]. The Show had been held at Down Farm, St. John's during the war years. The Show was one of the big annual events in the Calendar, together with Cricket Week. The Tunbridge Wells Motor Club held a Festival Rally, celebrating 50 years of Motoring.

The 1939-1945 additions to the War Memorial were unveiled by William, 1st. Viscount De L'Isle and Dudley, VC, KG, in July 1950. Again the British weather ran true to form and the August Bank Holiday, then the first weekend in August, was a washout.

The first Census since 1931 was held in 1951 and the population of Tunbridge Wells was recorded as 38,397, as against 35,367 in 1931 – a net increase of 3,030 people over 20 years, or an average of just over 150 people a year.

With the death of King George VI on 6th. February 1952, the accession of Queen Elizabeth II and her Coronation the following year on 2nd. June 1953, the long dark years of war and the post war years of austerity seemed to be over at last. People talked of a New Elizabethan Age and optimism was in the air. Only six years later, Harold Macmillan, the Prime Minister, could tell the electorate that 'you've never had it so good'. And that was largely true for Tunbridge Wells as well.

Calverley Road decorated for the Coronation, 1953.

CHAPTER 13

WORKING IT OUT
– FIFTY YEARS OF SHAPING THE FUTURE

by Philip Whitbourn

The late 1950s and early 1960s were not good times for the historic environment of Britain. In 1957, the Prime Minister of the day, Harold Macmillan, was telling a cheering rally in Bradford that "Most of our people have never had it so good". Inside England's homes, traditional chintzy "lived-in" interiors were giving way to the more angular and minimalist lines of the so-called "contemporary" style of décor. Outside, in towns and cities up and down the land, the post-war "International Style" of architecture was taking hold, with box-like steel-framed structures hung with glass "curtain walls", or clad with infill panels.

The 1950s had seen the introduction of the world's cheapest four-cylinder car, the Mini at £390 including tax, and in 1963 Dr Beeching's axe fell on a quarter of the country's rail network, severing the rail link between Tunbridge Wells and Brighton.

High profile demolition cases such as the Euston Arch and the Coal Exchange in London made national news, but a plea to the Prime Minister to intervene in such matters fell on deaf ears.

Decimus Burton's Calverley Market and Camden Inn, demolished in 1959...

...and replaced by National Provident House.

In Royal Tunbridge Wells, the end of the 1950s and the beginning of the 1960s was, sadly, marked by the destruction of Decimus Burton's former Market House and the Camden Inn at the corner of Camden and Calverley Roads.

However, as the 1960s wore on, the government became concerned about the rate at which architectural and townscape heritage was being lost. Thus, in 1967, Parliamentary time was found for the Civic

Amenities Act, which enabled Conservation Areas to be created, and in 1968 the present system of Listed Building Consents was introduced.

The driving force behind this latter measure was Lord Kennet, then Joint Parliamentary Secretary at the Ministry of Housing and Local Government, to whom all who care about the historic environment owe a debt of gratitude. Effectively, the 1968 Act gave all listed buildings the same measure of protection as that previously enjoyed by buildings that were the subject of Preservation Orders.

At that time, Tunbridge Wells formed part of Tonbridge Constituency, with Richard Hornby as its Member of Parliament. The first MP for Tunbridge Wells Constituency was Patrick Mayhew, later The Rt. Hon. Lord Mayhew of Twysden, who was elected in 1974. The question being asked in that year was "Who runs Britain – the Government or the miners?". Hardly a question on anyone's lips today. Patrick Mayhew was followed in 1997 by Archie Norman and in 2005 by Greg Clark.

In his maiden speech on 8th June 2005, Greg opened with the familiar Tunbridge Wells motto "Do well, doubt not". The Pantiles he described as one of the jewels of his constituency which 'will be at the heart of those celebrations of our 400th anniversary'. Greg concluded his maiden speech by saying: "You will probably have discerned from my remarks, Mr. Deputy Speaker, that I have fallen in love with Tunbridge Wells and its people. It is very easy to succumb to that. There is an old saying that 'Travel broadens the mind', but whenever I do travel these days I have cause to call to mind the final line from that great film 'Lawrence of Arabia': 'On the whole, I wish I'd stayed in Tunbridge Wells'."

The first Conservation Areas in Royal Tunbridge Wells were designated in 1969 by the Kent County Council, which was at that time the Local Planning Authority, and the boundaries were tightly drawn around The Pantiles and Calverley Park.

However, by 1974 the new Tunbridge Wells Council had taken over from the County Council as the Local Planning Authority. Local Government reorganisation gave rise to not a little discussion, both about the composition and names of the new authorities.

One idea was to amalgamate the town of Royal Tunbridge Wells with its smaller, but older, urban neighbour Tonbridge in a north-south direction. That, though, was discarded in favour of an east-west format, combining Royal Tunbridge Wells and Southborough with the Kentish countryside and villages along the Sussex border. Names canvassed for

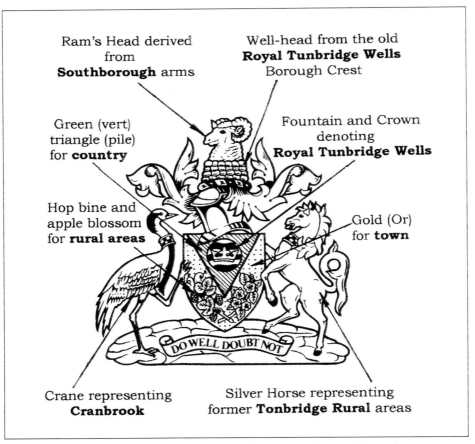

Ram's Head derived from **Southborough** arms

Well-head from the old **Royal Tunbridge Wells** Borough Crest

Green (vert) triangle (pile) for **country**

Fountain and Crown denoting **Royal Tunbridge Wells**

Hop bine and apple blossom for **rural areas**

Gold (Or) for **town**

DO WELL DOUBT NOT

Crane representing **Cranbrook**

Silver Horse representing former **Tonbridge Rural** areas

A symbolic representation of the amalgamation of town with country, and the bringing together of four former constituent authorities in the Tunbridge Wells Borough Council armorial bearings, granted on 2nd April 1976.

the new authority included "High Weald" but, eventually, the more readily identified name of Tunbridge Wells District was adopted, soon to be replaced by Tunbridge Wells Borough.

The armorial bearings granted to the then new Borough of Tunbridge Wells in 1976, illustrated on this page, perhaps serve to illustrate the aspiration to unite country and town, and to bring together Royal Tunbridge Wells, Southborough, Cranbrook and Tonbridge Rural areas into a single authority.

The new Tunbridge Wells District Council extended the separate Conservation Areas in Royal Tunbridge Wells to form a continuous one, covering more of the Town Centre. Further extensions in the Molyneux Park area followed in 1983, by which time the District Council had become the Borough Council. Broadwater Down was designated in 1989 and Pembury Road in 1992. the whole being consolidated into the present Royal Tunbridge Wells Conservation Area in the year 2000.

Alongside that welcome activity on the conservation front, the Authorities sought to shape the future of the town through a series of Local Development Plans. The first of these was the Kent County Council's 1962 Town Map, and a great disappointment it proved to be. One of its principal features was the denigrating of Camden Road, along with areas of houses to the east and west, as obsolete and "in urgent need of redevelopment", causing needless worry to owners of property there.

But worse was to come in 1966 from the former Royal Tunbridge Wells Corporation. The old Corporation, which existed before the Local Government reorganisation of 1972, was not the Local Planning Authority.

Nevertheless, in preparing its own Plan for the Town Centre, the Corporation consulted closely with the County Council, as the Local Planning Authority, to produce what it saw as a blueprint for the central part of Royal Tunbridge Wells. Among the proposals put forward were a fly-

Grant of Arms to Tunbridge Wells Borough Council, April 1976, received by the Mayor, Cllr. Myrtle Streeten.

over in Vale Road, rear goods access roads to the High Street shops and, most controversially of all, a one-way gyratory Inner Ring Road through, rather than around, the Town Centre. Lansdowne Road would have been one of the worst casualties of the scheme, with some houses demolished and others rendered unsuitable for residential purposes. Decimus Burton's former Victoria School building would have been another casualty.

In taking on the combined might of the Old Corporation and the County Council in a "David and Goliath" battle at a Public Inquiry in

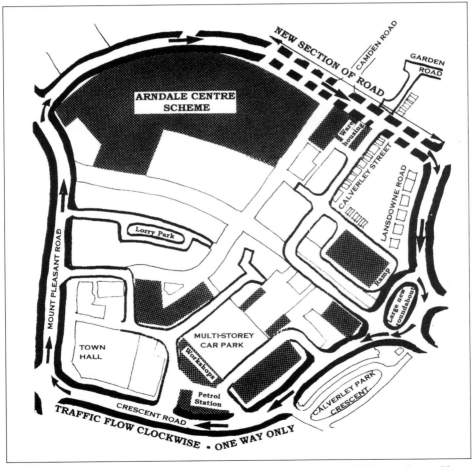

A Lucky Escape – the former Royal Tunbridge Wells Corporation 1966 Town Centre Plan, with its one-way gyratory ring-road through the town, was, fortunately, found wanting at a Public Inquiry held in 1970.

Victoria School Building.

1970, the Civic Society won the day, killing off this misconceived plan and, with it, a related scheme for an "Arndale Centre" where Royal Victoria Place now is. The Camden Road redevelopment envisaged in the 1962 Town Map was similarly killed off by the Society at another Public Inquiry in 1973, and a General Improvement area was established instead. Such events have proved to be landmarks in the shaping of the town's future and, although the Civic Society did not make itself popular in official circles during those times, later generations of planners have felt more appreciative of the stand taken by the Society in these matters.

Modified and discredited, the 1962 Town Map lingered on through the 1970s, well past its "sell-by" date. With a view to providing background information for a new Plan for Royal Tunbridge Wells and Southborough, the Borough Council produced a series of "Topic Reports" in the late 1970s on Housing, Employment, Recreation and Tourism, Shopping, Transport, Townscape and Conservation.

The Plan itself emerged in 1984, but was not adopted until 1988, following a major Public Inquiry in 1985. An unfortunate effect of the reorganisation of Local government in 1974 was that the town of Royal Tunbridge Wells was the only part of the new authority that was left without a voice through a Town or Parish Council. Some effort was made in 1977 to remedy that situation through the setting up by the Borough Council of a 'Community Forum'. The initiative, however, proved short-lived, and it has fallen to the Civic Society to fill the gap in the system. Whether recent fresh initiatives concerning a Town Forum will fare better, remains to be seen.

One of the main issues for the Society at that hearing was a successful bid to save the tree-lined Pembury Road from a series of 120 ft diameter

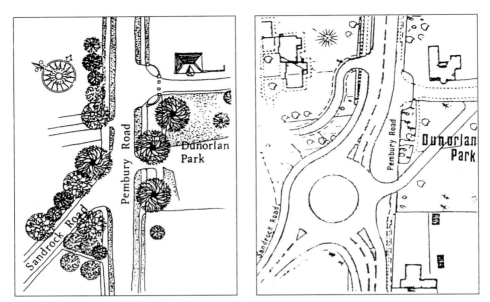

Left: the junction of Pembury and Sandrock Roads.
Right: Kent County Council's proposed scheme, dropped following the 1985 Public Inquiry.
(Both illustrations to scale)

roundabouts, proposed by the County Council, together with a new roadway planned to run diagonally across the entrance to Robert Marnock's Dunorlan Park.

During the quarter of a century or so that elapsed between the 1962 Town Map and the 1988 Adopted Plan, various development schemes came and went. New developments that materialised included the Pump Room development at the southern end of The Pantiles, the Eden House and Walmer House developments on Mount Sion, and new office blocks in Lonsdale Gardens and Church Road off Mount Pleasant.

Buildings that survived threats or faced uncertain futures included Decimus Burton's Trinity Church, now Trinity Arts Centre; Jerningham House on Mount Sion; The Corn Exchange and Nos. 1-5 The Pantiles; the Wellington Hotel and Bredbury on Mount Ephraim; Decimus Burton's Calverley Hotel, now the Hotel du Vin; No.2 Calverley Park, and the Congregational Church, now Habitat, and the Opera House on Mount Pleasant.

The loss of any one of these local landmarks would have been bad enough but, had they all been allowed to go the cumulative effect upon the character of the town would have been very serious indeed. Another local landmark that was spared was the clock tower of the Central Station, which was reprieved when a scheme for a shopping precinct with thirty shops over the tracks was dropped in 1968.

The 1984 version of the Local Plan envisaged an increase in shopping floorspace in the Calverley Road/Victoria Road area of 100,000 sq.ft. (9,300 sq.m.). Significantly, the Plan nevertheless added that "the local Planning Authority would have to be satisfied that such an increase would not have adverse effects on existing shopping facilities".[1]

Such, however, can be the separation of the twin processes of forward planning and development control that, in 1985, Tunbridge Wells' biggest-ever shopping project was being worked up alongside the Local Plan, but without much evidence of co-ordination between the two. The eventual result was Royal Victoria Place, which opened in 1992 with shopping floorspace more than double that provided for in the 1984 Local Plan.

Not surprisingly, therefore, continuing anxieties arose over the 2002 Local Plan Review, concerning the possible effect of further extensions to Royal Victoria Place. In an age where town centres generally are being criticised as "cloned", with ubiquitous multiple stores up and down the land, Tunbridge Wells still remains fortunate in having a number of individual shops of distinctive character.

"God moves in a mysterious way", in the words of the eighteenth century poet William Cowper, and seldom more so in Tunbridge Wells than through the 1966 Bishop of Rochester's Commission on churches in the Deanery.

This proposed that Trinity Church should be recognised as the official parish church of Tunbridge Wells and that Christ Church, situated a short distance from the historic Church of King Charles the Martyr, should be declared redundant.[2] In the event, Trinity was declared redundant in 1972 and converted into an Arts Centre, while Christ Church has been demolished and a new Church Centre built on its site. The old Catholic Church of St.Augustine in Grosvenor Road was demolished too, and a new Catholic Church, which has been listed as Grade II, was opened in Crescent Road in 1975 to the designs of Maguire and Murray. The former Congregational Church in Mount Pleasant still stands, however, albeit now converted into a Habitat store.

The reduced need for church accommodation, and the increased demand for shopping floor space, is but one trend that has been

Molyneux Place, Mount Ephraim, previously the Reliance Insurance Offices, the Earl's Court Hotel and the residence of Hon. F. G. Molyneux.

observable during recent decades. During the 1960s and 1970s, there was much pressure for office development. Recently, however, the trend has been for the replacement of offices with residential accommodation. Molyneux Place on Mount Ephraim is one example of this and Garden House in Calverley Street is another. Pressure for redevelopment as housing is strong, too, on many existing residential properties. Houses in pleasant gardens are known in the planning world as 'brown-field sites'. Often, however, they are not brown at all, but a shade of green that has resulted from mature planting and established trees. Worrying changes can thus result from such redevelopment, especially outside the designated Conservation Areas.

Not all aspects of civilised life, of course, fall within the ambit of the Town Planning system. Law and Order issues, for instance, graffiti, the frequency of refuse collection, and management regimes for parks, open spaces, schools, hospitals, public transport and other faiclities, are but a few examples of matters which can affect us all, but which normally lie outside the direct control of the Town Planning system. Nevertheless, we remain reliant on the Planning system to provide that basic framework for the proper conservation of this historic town, and the right blueprint for its future.

In 2004 the government changed the planning system, replacing Local Plans with "Local Development Frameworks" prepared within a much wider Regional Context, instead of a county-wide one.

In March 2005, Kent Life writer Dr Diana Crampton described Tunbridge Wells as "undoubtedly Kent's most elegant town".[3] This elegance may, in some measure, be attributed to the efforts of our Planners, on occasion, but it is certainly, in no small measure, the result of our Planners not always getting their way. The challenge for them in future will be to ensure that this shining reputation the town has for elegance is maintained far into Tunbridge Wells' fifth century and beyond.

*Frontispiece of 'Tunbridge Wells; or, A Day's Courtship',
by Thomas Rawlins, 1678. The satiric nature of the play
can be seen by the names of the characters in it –
Tom Fairlove (Our Hero), Owmuch, Sir Lofty Vaniman,
Squire Fop, Alderman Paywel, Parson Quibble
and Poet Witless.*

NOTES, REFERENCES AND BIBLIOGRAPHY

In general, the following locations are prime depositaries for material in this monograph:

Tunbridge Wells Reference Library

Tunbridge Wells Museum

Centre for Kentish Studies (CKS) at Maidstone

East Sussex Records Office (ESRO) at Lewes

For many chapters, the following are specific sources. Consequently, they are generally not repeated in the individual Chapter listings below.

PRIMARY SOURCES

Lord Dudley North: A Forest of Vanities, London 1645

Thomas Rawlins: Tunbridge Wells; or A Day's Courtship, a Comedy. London 1678

Thomas Benge Burr: The History of Tunbridge Wells. London, 1766

Sprange: Tunbridge Wells Guides, 1780-1809

Paul Amsinck: Tunbridge Wells and its neighbourhood 1810

John Britton: Descriptive Sketches of Tunbridge Wells. John Britton, London. 1832

Maps: Symondson, 1597; Bowra, 1738; Sprange, 1775; Burrows 1808; Billings (Britton) 1832; Stidolph, 1838; Colbran 1839, 1845 & 1851; Gisborne, 1849; Clifford, 1855; Brackett 1868

Ordnance Survey maps, 1867, 1897, 1909 and 1938

Population Censuses, 1831-1931, 1951-2001

Tunbridge Wells Planning Applications Index 1867-1891; 1891-1913

Kelly's Kent Directory – various dates

Kelly's Directories for Tunbridge Wells – various dates

Kent & Sussex (Tunbridge Wells) Courier – various dates

Pelton's Guides and Directories – various dates

Property Sale catalogues (held in Reference Library)

SECONDARY SOURCES

Margaret Barton: Tunbridge Wells. Faber & Faber, London. 1937

Sue Brown: Researching Tunbridge Wells, RTWCS LHG 2003

Willard Connely: Beau Nash. Werner Laurie, London.1955

Roger Farthing : History of Mount Sion, 2003

Lewis Melville: Society at Tunbridge Wells. In the 18th. Century and After. Eveleigh Nash, London 1912

Nikolaus Pevsner: The Buildings of England: West Kent and the Weald by John Newman: 2nd. Edition: Penguin Books 1976

Alan Savidge: Royal Tunbridge Wells [1st edition] 1975

And for individual chapters, the following are specific primary and secondary sources and references:

Chapter 1 The Origins of the High Weald and its Iron Industry

The South-East. Down and Weald: Kent, Surrey and Sussex: John Talbot White. Eyre Methuen, 1977

Royal Tunbridge Wells, Past and Present: ed. JCM Given, Courier Printing & Publishing, 1946

Weald of Kent and Sussex: Sheila Kaye-Smith. Robert Hale, 1953

The Kent & Sussex Weald: Peter Brandon. Phillimore, 2003

The Iron Industry of the Weald: Henry Cleere & David Crossley. Leicester University Press, 1985
Iron for the Eagles: The Iron Industry of Roman Britain: David Sim & Isabel Ridge. Tempus, 2002
Burke's Peerage and Baronetage 1910.

Chapter 2 Baths, Holy Wells and Spas

The English Spa 1560-1815. A Social History: Phyllis Hembry. The Athlone Press, 1990
Aquae Britannia: Rediscovering 17th. Century Springs and Spas in the Footsteps of Celia Fiennes: Bruce Osborne & Cora Weaver. Cora Weaver, 1996
The Inland Resorts and Spas of Britain: Frederick Alderson. David & Charles, 1973
Dictionary of National Biography. OUP 1975 and 2004.
Burke's Peerage and Baronetage 1910.

Chapter 3 The Queen's Wells

[1] The History of Tunbridge Wells, Thomas Benge Burr, 1766, p.16
[2] The National Archives reference MPI 1/68
[3] ibid. reference SC.12/18/60
[4] Benge Burr, op.cit. p.311
[5] Royal Tunbridge Wells, Alan Savidge, 1975, p.27
[6] Seventh Report of The Royal Commission on Historical Manuscripts, Part I Report and Appendix
[7] Letters of John Chamberlain: 2 vols. American Philosophical Society,1939
[8] The English Spa 1560-1815. A Social History. By Phyllis Hembry, Athlone Press,1990,p.46
[9] The Queens Welles, Dr. L. Rowzee, 1656 ed, p.55
[10] Luttrell Ms. Travell 13th, 1680
[11] ibid.
[12] Benge Burr, op.cit. p.31
[13] Rowzee, op.cit.. p.56
[14] Rowzee,op.cit.
[15] Memoirs of the Comte de Gramont by Anthony Hamilton: George Routledge & Sons, Ltd. London. 1930.

Chapter 4 The Rise of Mount Sion

[1] Benge Burr, op.cit. p.45
[2] Society at Tunbridge Wells, in the Eighteenth Century – and after, Lewis Melville, p.229.

Chapter 5 Georgian High Noon

The Tunbridge Wells Guide: published by Jasper Sprange: 1780-1809
The Illustrated Journeys of Celia Fiennes 1685-1712. Ed. by Christopher Morris. Macdonald & Co. 1982
General View of Agriculture of County of Sussex. by Rev. Arthur Young. London. 1813

Transport and Economy. The Turnpike Roads of Eighteenth Century Britain. by Eric Pawson. Academic Press, 1977

The English Spa 1560-1815. A Social History. by Phyllis Hembry. Athlone Press, 1990

A Tour through the Whole Island of Great Britain by Daniel Defoe. Everyman's Library, 1962

Road Transport and Economic Growth in the 18th. Century. By John Chartres. Refresh 9, 1989

Chapter 6 1789 to 1825 –The End of an Era?

[1] Evans, John *An Excursion to Brighton ... A Visit to Tunbridge Wells and A Trip to Southend.* 1821 p 283

[2] Evans. Op cit Description of Brighton between pages 33 and 72.

[3] Evans. Op cit p 123

[4] Quoted in Melville, Lewis *Society at Tunbridge Wells in the 18th century – and after* 1912 p 227

[5] Amsinck, Paul *Tunbridge Wells and its neighbourhood* 1810 p 32

[6] Melville op cit p 275

[7] Evans op cit pp 140, 138 and 139

[8] Tunbridge Wells Museum

[9] Evans op cit pp 157 and 190

[10] Sprange, J The Tunbridge Wells Guide 1808 p 99

[11] Various sources. Roger Farthing in his notes to Royal Tunbridge Wells: A Pictorial History corrects earlier reporters who quote 1793, but his reference to the Maidstone Journal may be one week too early.

[12] CKS P371e/8/2-3

[13] Amsinck op cit pp 33, 34

[14] Sprange 1808 Guide pp 34 to 38. Earlier guides include the numerous testimonials.

[15] Barton, Margaret Tunbridge Wells 1937 p 4

[16] Tunbridge Wells Museum. Sprange Collection.

[17] Amsinck op cit p 19

[18] Tunbridge Wells Museum. Sprange Collection.

[19] Brackett, Arthur William Tunbridge Wells through the centuries 1928 p33

[20] Tunbridge Wells Museum. Sprange Collection.

[21] Cumberland, Richard Memoirs 1806 pp 524, 525

[22] Tunbridge Wells Museum. Sprange Collection.

[23] Tunbridge Wells Museum. Sprange Collection.

[24] Tunbridge Wells Museum. Sprange Collection

[25] Quoted in Melville op cit pp 275, 276

[26] Amsinck op cit p 108

[27] Savidge, Alan Royal Tunbridge Wells 1975 p 116

[28] Amsinck op cit p 41

[29] Tunbridge Wells Museum. Sprange Collection

[30] Tunbridge Wells Museum. Sprange Collection

[31] Tunbridge Wells Museum. Sprange Collection

[32] Sprange's guides include lists of the rooms available to visitors. 1786 – 418, 1808 – 472, 1811 – 490, 1817 – 706, 1822 (Clifford) – 658. Note that the classification of rooms changed from 1817 onwards, so the figures may not be directly comparable.

[33] CKS U840/C3/11

[34] Farthing, Roger *The Jerningham Letters* part 3 RTWCS Newsletter Spring 2000
[35] Tunbridge Wells Museum. Sprange Collection
[36] Amsinck op cit pp 27, 28
[37] Brackett op cit p55 and Melville op cit p 277
[38] Amsinck op cit p 17
[39] CKS U909/C94/3

Chapter 7 Calverley New Town

[1] *Colbran's New Guide for Tunbridge Wells* 1844, page 48
[2] ibid
[3] *Joseph Bramah – A Century of Invention 1749-1851* Ian McNeil, page 175
[4] CKS, U 2737
[5] *Descriptive Sketches of Tunbridge Wells and the Calverley Estate 1832* John Britton FSA, page 44
[6] *Tunbridge Wells Visitor*, vol.3, No.17, 1834, page 255
[7] Colbran, op.cit, page 49
[8] Obituary in The Tunbridge Wells Gazette, Friday 12th February 1875

Chapter 8 The Growth of Population and the Local Economy, and the Rule of the Commissioners, 1830-1889

[1] JFC Harrison *The Early Victorians* p.
[2] Kentish Gazette 8.10.1830, *Government and Politics in Kent 1640-19J4* p. 117
[3] C.W.Chalklin, *Estate Development and the beginnings of Modern Tunbridge Wells* Arch.Cant. 1934, p335
[4] C. W. Chalklin 'The Towns' from the *Economy of Kent 1640-1914* Ed. G. Armstrong
[5] A. Savidge *Royal Tunbridge Wells* p. 92
[6] P.Hastings, *Crime and Public Order from Government and Politics in Kent* Ed. F. Lansberry p.213
[7] P. Hastings op. cit., p.238
[8] A. Savidge op. cit,p. 125
[9] P.Whitboum *Decimus Burton Esq, Architect and Gentleman (1800-1881)* p.23
[10] A. Savidge op. cit, p. 125
[11] Minute Book No .620. Tunbridge Wells Borough Archives.
[12] A. Savidge op.cit. p. 167

Chapter 9 The Railway and Tunbridge Wells (1846-2005)

South Eastern Railway, by Adrian Gray M.A. Pub: Middleton Press 1990
South Eastern & Chatham Railways by Adrian Gray, M.A. Pub: Middleton Press 1998
Southern Main Lines – Tonbridge to Hastings by Vic Mitchell & Keith Smith. Middleton Press 1987
Branch Lines to Tunbridge Wells by Vic Mitchell & Keith Smith. Middleton Press 1986
Maunsell's SR Steam Carriage Stock by David Gould. Oakwood Press 3rd edition 2000
Kent & Sussex Courier – in particular, several editions in summer 1878

Chapter 10 Canon Hoare and the Victorian Ecclesiastical Scene

[1] *The Countess of Huntingdon and her Connexion* edited by the Rev. J.B. Figgis (1891) and *The Coronet and the Cross* by the Rev. A.H. New (1857).
[2] This and other biographical quotations are from *Edward Hoare M.A.* by the Rev. J.H. Townsend, D.D., 1896.
[3] *The Centenary History of St. Peter's* by the Rev. John W. Hurst.
[4] *Royal Tunbridge Wells* by Alan Savidge, 1975.
[5] see Archbishop Tait's papers at Lambeth Palace Library.
[6] in a letter from the Rev. C.R. Pearson to the Ecclesiastical Commissioners (Lambeth Palace Library).
[7] *The life of Archbishop Benson* by A.C. Benson, 1900.

Chapter 11 Fighting For The Future

A Memoir of the late John Stone-Wigg, Kent & Sussex Courier, 1897
The Jubilee of Tunbridge Wells as an Incorporated Borough, C H Strange, Tunbridge Wells Corporation, 1939
Tunbridge Wells Improvement Act, 1890
Tunbridge Wells Borough Council minutes (Tunbridge Wells Museum)
Tunbridge Wells Borough Council press cuttings books (Tunbridge Wells Museum)
Tunbridge Wells Chamber of Trade press cuttings books (Tunbridge Wells Museum)

Chapter 12 The Second World War and its Aftermath: 1939 – 1953

Minutes of the Chamber of Trade 1939 – 1945
Minutes of the Council's Emergency Committee 1939 – 1945
Tunbridge Wells Local Youth Committee minutes 1940 – 1946
Enemy Action in Kent, compiled by the County Civil Defence Dept.
Diaries of Brig. Manley – Sims re: Home Guard
Sprange Diaries from 1939
Civil Defence War Diaries
Collection of Posters WW II 1940 – 1945 at University of Nottingham Library Manuscript Dept
WHO WAS WHO [names associated with Tunbridge Wells in the years 1939 – 1952]
Oxford Dictionary of National Biography [New Edition, 2004]
THE TIMES 'Obituaries'
Tunbridge Wells Courier for years 1939 – 1952
The Courier 'Battle of Flying Bombs' special publication 15 September 1944
'Civil Defence' special edition booklet [gives names of casualties)

H. S. Banner	Kentish Fire	
H. E. Bates	Flying Bombs Over England	
	Froglets of Westerham	1994
D. Bennet	Hand Book of Kent Defences	1977
H. R. Pratt Boorman	Kent Unconquered – Kent Messenger	1951
Susan Briggs	Keep Smiling Through,	
	the Home Front 1939 – 1945	1975
Mike Brown	Christmas on the Home Front	2004
	After the Battle	
Frank Chapman	Warwick Column in the Courier	
	various dates	

Richard Cobb	Still Life	1983
Emma Crocker	The Home Front	
Bernard Darwin	War on the line S.E. Railway Co.	1946
Keith Gulvin	Kent Homeguard	
Peter Hayward	For the Sake of the Children	
S. Hylton	From Rationing tc Rock, the 1950's revisited	1998
S. Hylton	Kent and Sussex 1940	2004
S. Hylton	Their darkest hour	pub?
Anthony James	Informing the people [list of HMSO publications for WW2]	1996
Alan Jenkins	The Forties	1977
J. D. Lewis	W.V.S. in Kent 1939 – 1945	1947
Norman Longmate	How we lived then	1971
S. P. Mackenzie	The Homeguard	OUP 1995
Alec McGowen	Young Gemini	1979
James McMillan	The Way it Changed 1951 – 1975	1987
Kenneth Morgan	The Peoples Peace – history since 1945	OUP 1999
Bob Ogley	Doodlebugs and Rockets	1992
	Kent at War	
V. Sackville West	The Women's Land Army	1944
G. Scott Page	Recollections of a provincial dental surgeon	1984
W. L. Platts	KCC Admin. in War 1939 – 1945	1946
Harry Pratley	A Bookseller remembers	1990
Andrew Rootes	Front-line County: Robert Hale Ltd.	1980
Shire Books	The Home Front	2002
Joyce Shoebridge	Growing up in St. Peters	2001
Fred Sibbey	Fred Sibbey's story	1996
H. Spalding Ed.	Tunbridge Wells, a report	1945
F. C. Squirrell	Civil Defence in Tunbridge Wells	
	Civil Defence a history of the Borough	1939-1945
R. S. Turnball	My Tunbridge Wells Story	1988
Kent Aviation H. R. S.	Buzz Bomb Diary	
	We'll meet again	
Kent Zone Homeguard	Its early days 1940 – 41. Booklet: Tonbridge Reference Library	
Ed. Calder & Sheridan	Speak for yourself	
	[Anthology 1937 – 1949]	1984
	Policing in Kent 1800 – 2000 Phillimore	2002

Tunbridge Wells 2nd Selection Rowland and Beavis   1994
ESCC, History of, 1889 – 1974 C.R.V. Bell. Phillimore   1975
Notes from W.V.S. in Kent 1939 – 1945 by J. D. Lewis, published by Kent Messenger [no date]

Chapter 13 Working It Out – Fifty Years of Shaping the Future

[1] Royal Tunbridge Wells and Southborough Local Plan Deposit Copy, 1984, page 149.
[2] Kent and Sussex Courier, 29th April 1966, page 1
[3] Tunbridge Wells Life, March 2005, page 14

ACKNOWLEDGMENTS

The publishers have sought to establish the copyright holders of all illustrations in this monograph. If they have failed unwittingly, they offer their apologies and will rectify their mistake in any reprint.

Many old prints, maps and postcards prior to the 20th. century are generally, by their very age, out of copyright; and since each can be found in a number of public and private collections, it is not realistic to attribute any one collection as a source or copyright holder.

But we would like to acknowledge the following as the sources for many of the illustrations reproduced in this book:

The Tunbridge Wells Museum and Art Gallery, and particularly for the Kip engraving of 1719, the Loggon print of 1748 and the illustrations in Chapter 8 and 11;

The Tunbridge Wells Reference Library, particularly for many early photographs of both people and places in Tunbridge Wells and for the illustrations in Chapter 12;

The Tunbridge Wells Courier, for historic photographs from their Archives, particularly in Chapter 12;

The Kent Messenger, for historic photographs from their Archives.

We would like to thank them all for permission to reproduce from the copies they own.

We would also like to make the following specific acknowledgements:

The map in Chapter 1 of the High Weald was designed by John Talbot White and drawn by Neil Hyslop and is reproduced from The South-East. Down and Weald: Kent, Surrey and Sussex: John Talbot White. Eyre Methuen, 1977.

The map in Chapter 1 'Distribution of Ironworks in the Weald', by Sue Rowland, is reproduced from Peter Brandon, The Kent and Sussex Weald (2003) by permission of the publisher, Phillimore & Co. Ltd, Shopwyke Manor Barn, Chichester, West Sussex, PO20 2BG Website: www.phillimore.co.uk.

The miniature of Dudley, Lord North in Chapter 2 is courtesy of Christies and Phillimore & Co. and was previously published by them in 'Royal Tunbridge Wells. A Pictorial History' by the late Roger Farthing.

The maps of the Wybarne estates and the Pantiles in Chapter 3, of Mount Sion in Chapter 4, and of 19th.century Tunbridge Wells, Calverley New Town and the Residential Parks of Tunbridge Wells in Chapter 7, have been specially drawn for this publication by Dr. Philip Whitbourn, to whom we extend our grateful thanks.

The Turnpike Map of 1806 in Chapter 5 supplied by courtesy of Steve Clark, www.theoldmapshop.com

The photograph of the Tunbridge Wells Police Force in 1874 in Chapter 8 is taken with permission from 'Policing in Kent 1800 – 2000' by Roy Ingleton, published by Phillimore & Co. in 2002.

The photograph in Chapter 9 of Tunbridge Wells Station in 1891 is the copyright of the Tonbridge Historical Society, whose permission to reproduce is gratefully acknowledged.

The print of Tunbridge Wells Station c.1850 in Chapter 9 is the copyright of the Ironbridge Gorge Museum Trust, whose permission to reproduce is gratefully acknowledged.

The plan of the 'Wilderness' development and the photograph of a flooded 'Wilderness' tunnel in Chapter 12 are reproduced by permission of Nick Catford and 'Subterranea Britannica'.

The conversion of historic prices into equivalent 2005 values has been achieved using the Conversion Tables available in the Tunbridge Wells Reference Library.

NOTES ON CONTRIBUTORS

Lionel Anderson has lived in Tunbridge Wells since 1964. A retired investment manager, he spent most of his working life in the City of London, managing company pension schemes and Charitable Endowments. Since retirement, he has continued to advise various charities on their investments and has completed a study in Kentish History at the University of Kent. He is a liveryman in the Turners Company and a Freeman of the City of London.

John Arkell has lived most of his life in West Kent. After attending Sevenoaks School, early training as a surveyor was followed by appointments with local precision engineering businesses. A keen interest in railways and modelmaking has lead to an increasing amount of research in the railways of West Kent. A life member and regular volunteer at Horsted Keynes on the Bluebell Railway, he is also Chairman of the Orpington & District Model Railway Society and a member of the Historical Model Railway Society and the South Eastern & Chatham Society.

Anne Bates was born and has lived all her life in Tunbridge Wells. After leaving Blackheath High School, she studied Art at the Tunbridge Wells School of Art and in London at the Central School of Arts and Crafts (now St. Martin's Central School). She worked as a florist and after retiring, has researched local and family history. She is a granddaughter of Thomas Bates (1864-1930), who built many houses in Warwick Park, and Roedean, Blatchington and Forest Roads at the beginning of the 20th. century. She was a contributor of three chapters of 'The Residential Parks of Tunbridge Wells'.

Dr Ian Beavis read Classics at the University of Exeter, researching entomology in the ancient world. He is a native of Tunbridge Wells, and is currently Collections Management Officer at Tunbridge Wells Museum and Art Gallery. He is co-author of 'Tunbridge Wells in Old Photographs', 'Tunbridge Wells in Old Photographs – A Second Selection' and 'Tunbridge Wells and Rusthall Commons – A History and Natural History'. He regularly gives talks and guided walks featuring local history and natural history.

Geoffrey Copus has lived in Tunbridge Wells since 1960. Geoffrey's main interest is the history of the church and parish of St. Barnabas. He collaborated with the late Roger Farthing in cataloguing the extensive residual archives of the Manor of Rusthall before these were deposited at the Centre for Kentish Studies. He, and his wife Brenda, were contributors of three chapters of 'The Residential Parks of Tunbridge Wells'.

John Cunningham read History at Peterhouse, Cambridge and has written several local histories, including 'The Origins of Warwick Park'. His career was essentially in Marketing in the advertising, market research and publishing industries. Now retired, he is Vice-Chairman of the Royal Tunbridge Wells Civic Society and Hon. Secretary of its Local History Group. He was the Editor and a contributor of five chapters of 'The Residential Parks of Tunbridge Wells'.

Chris Jones read History at the University of Warwick. He met his wife, Charmian, while they were both studying in Venice. They have lived in Tunbridge Wells since 1981 and been members of the Civic Society for most of that time. Chris has worked in IT for nearly thirty years. He is currently analysing a system for archiving material broadcast by the BBC World Service. Chris has been Editor of the Civic Society Newsletter for the last six years.

Dr. Philip Whitbourn OBE, FSA, FRIBA is a qualified architect who, before retirement, held the post of Chief Architect at English Heritage and then the post of Secretary to the International Council on Monuments and Sites. Now retired, he is President of the Royal Tunbridge Wells Civic Society, of which he was a founder member in 1959. He is Chairman of the Local History Group of the Society and author of the Group's first monograph entitled 'Decimus Burton. Architect and Gentleman.' He is also part-author with Cecil Beeby of the Group's third monograph entitled 'The Skinners' School. Its controversial birth and its landmark buildings'; and contributed one chapter to 'The Residential Parks of Tunbridge Wells'.

INDEX

Armorial bearings of Tunbridge Wells Borough Council.